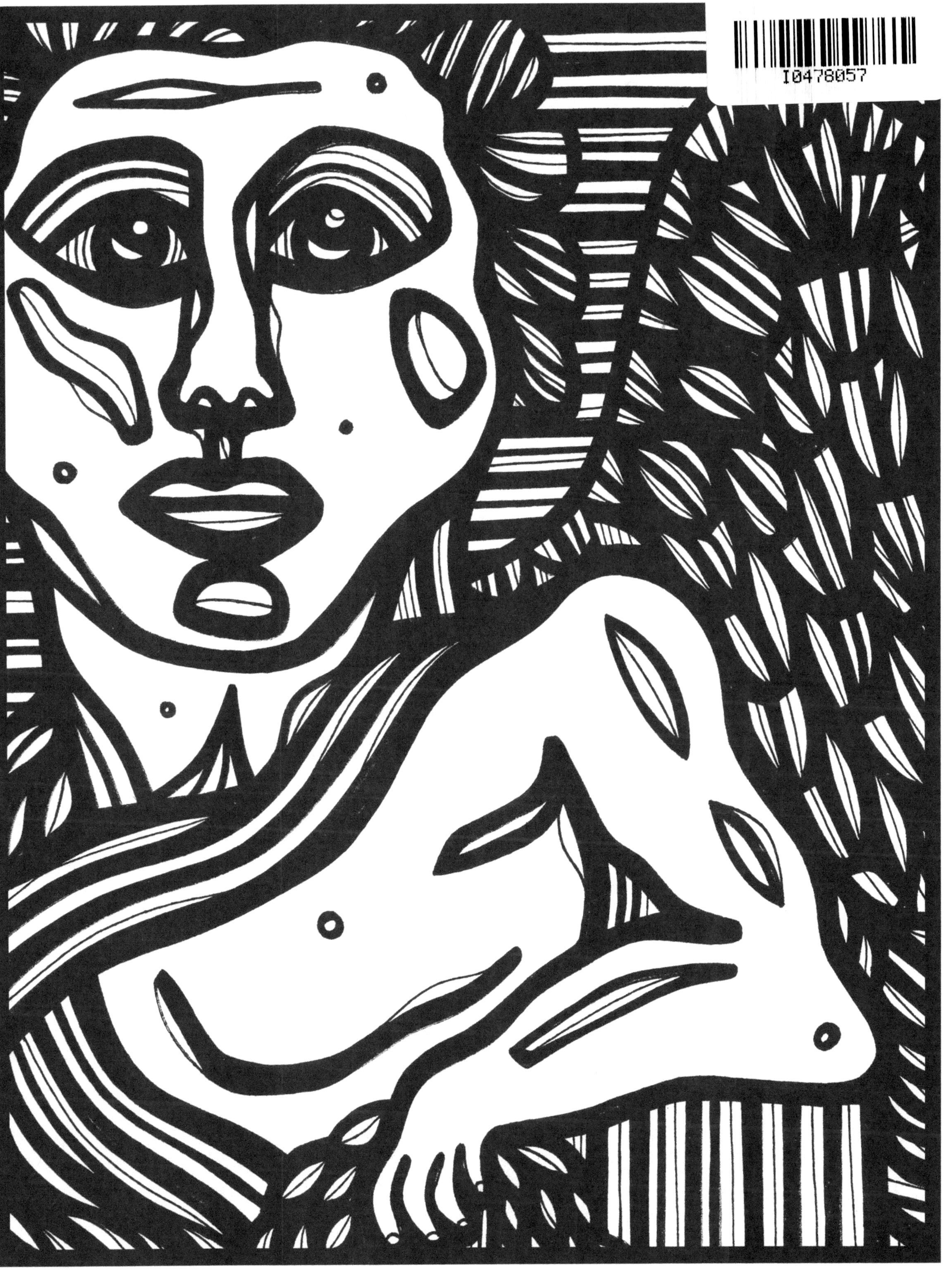

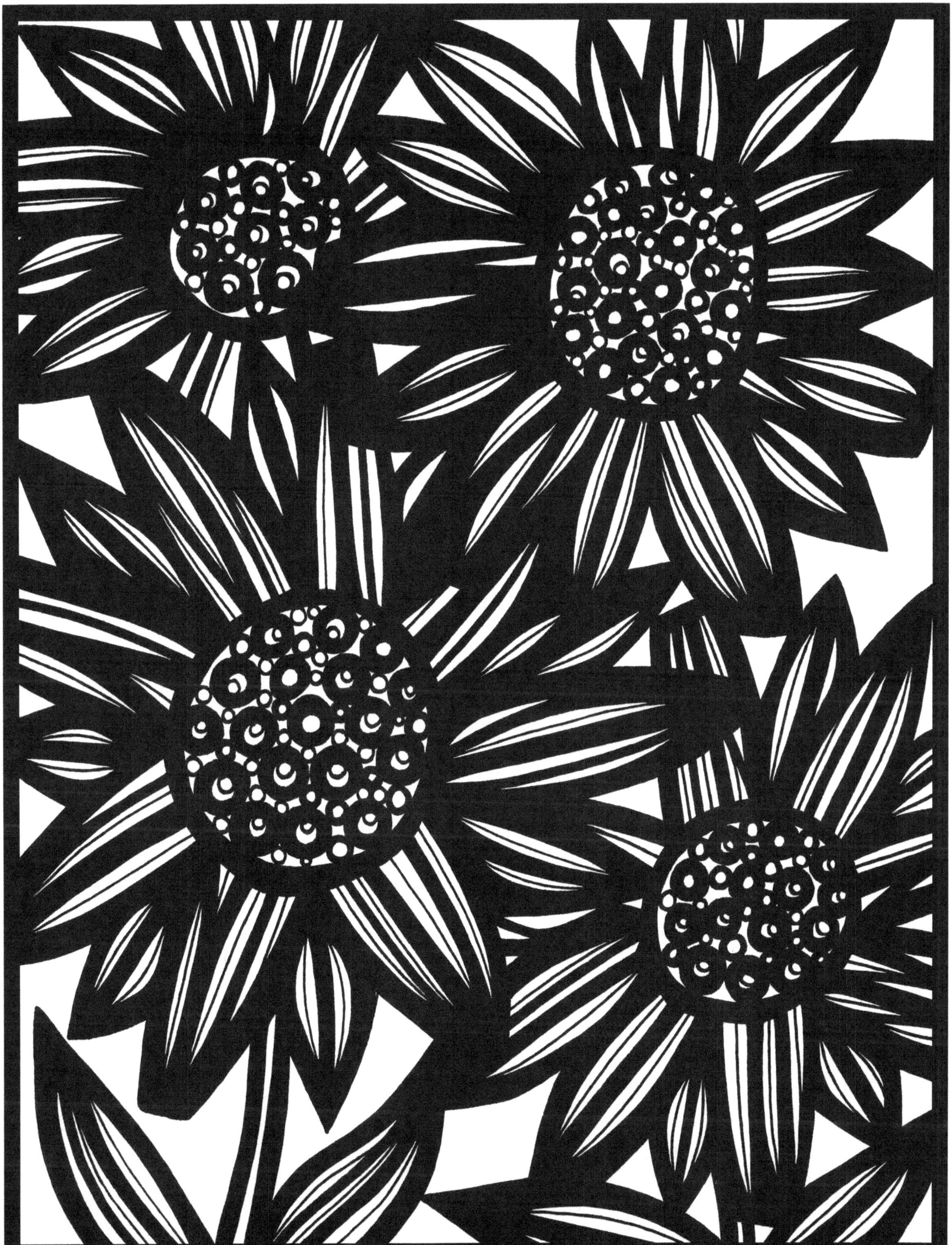

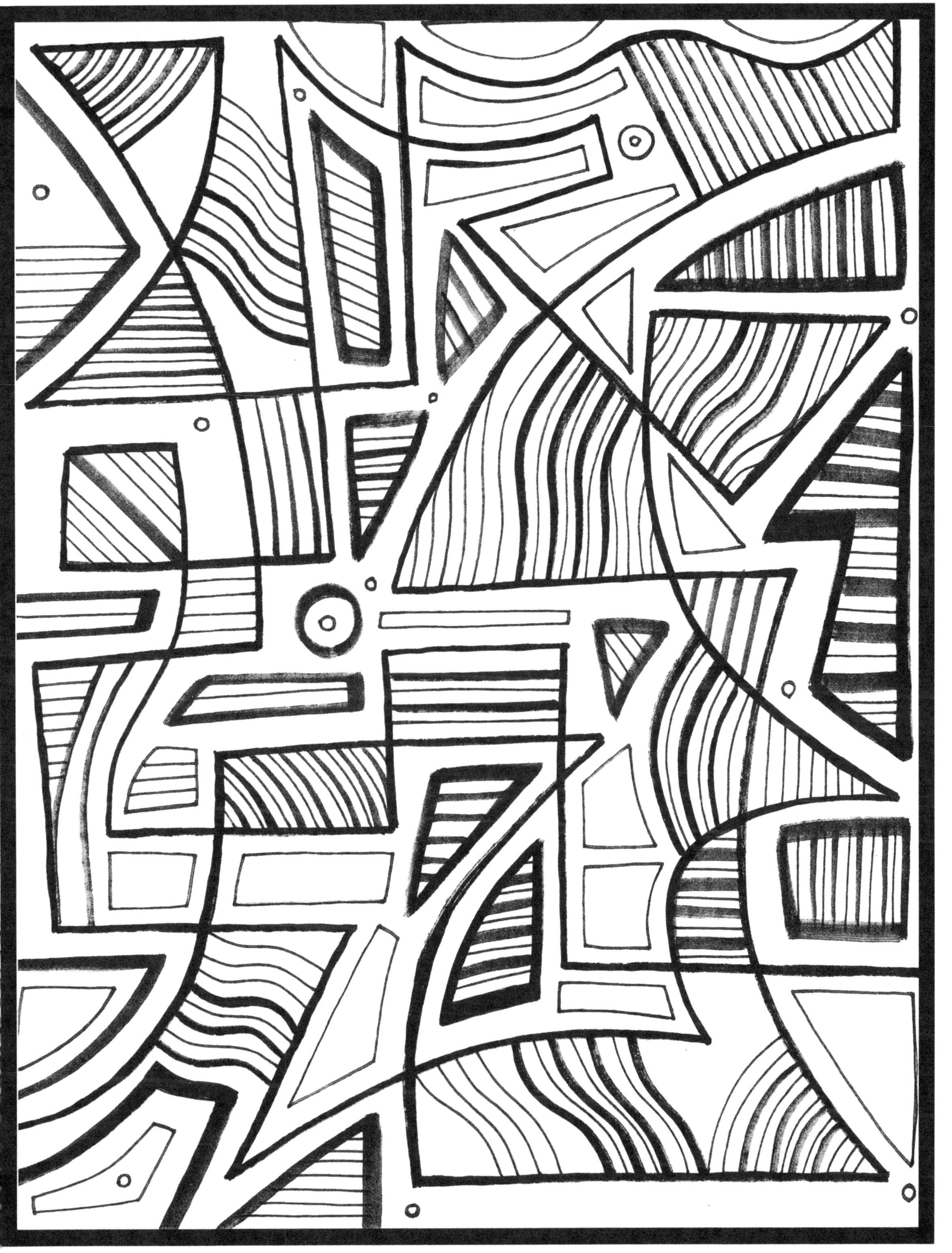

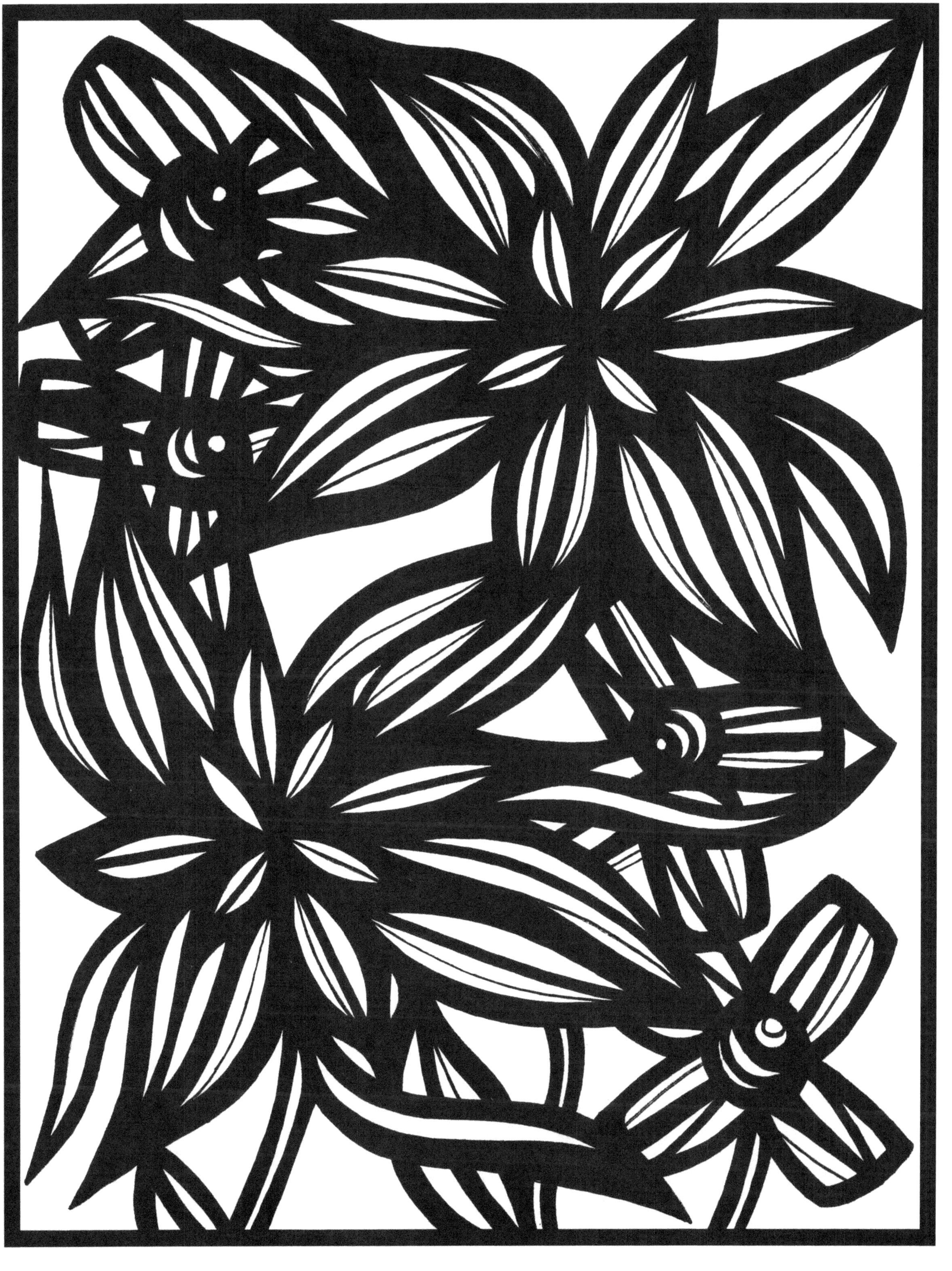

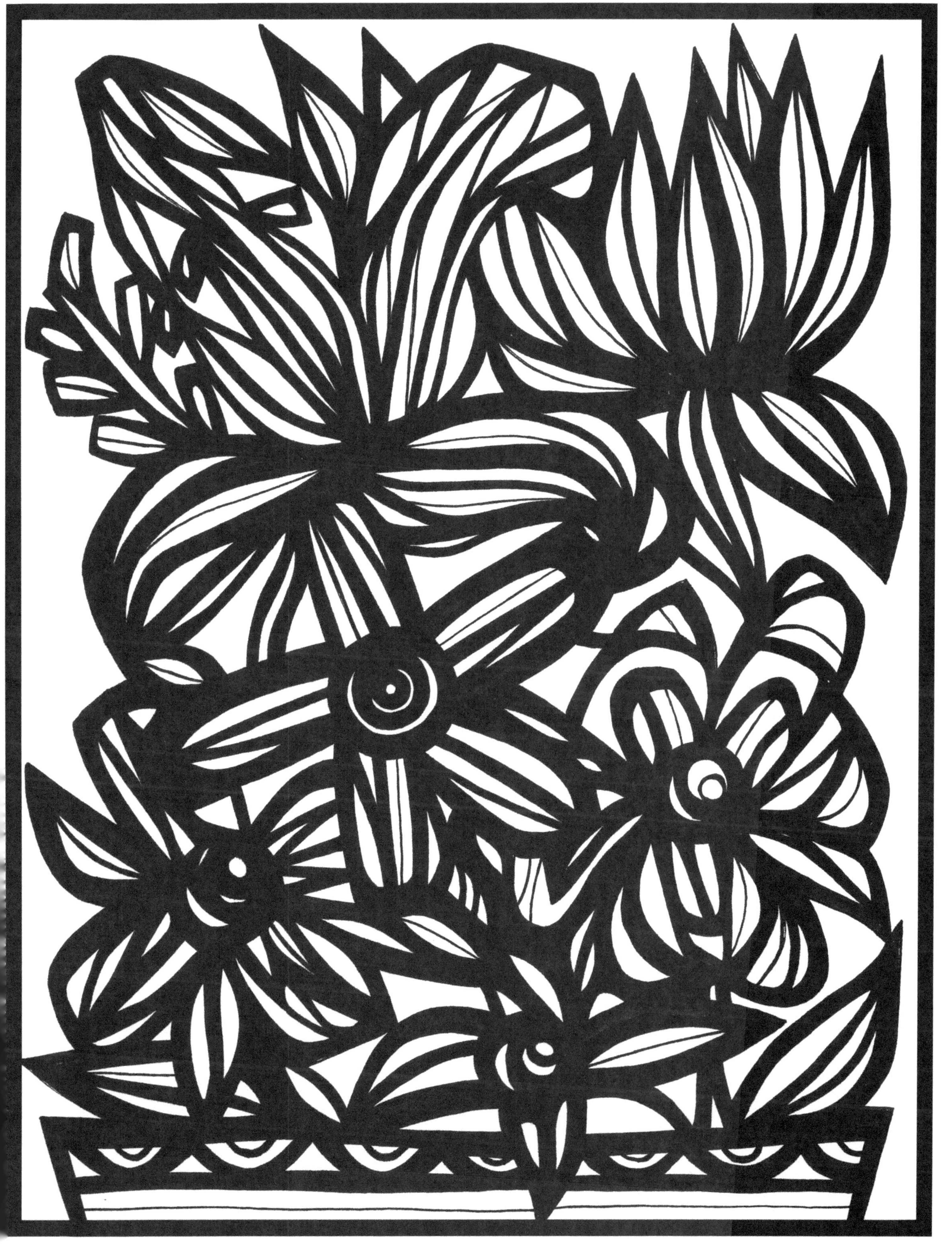

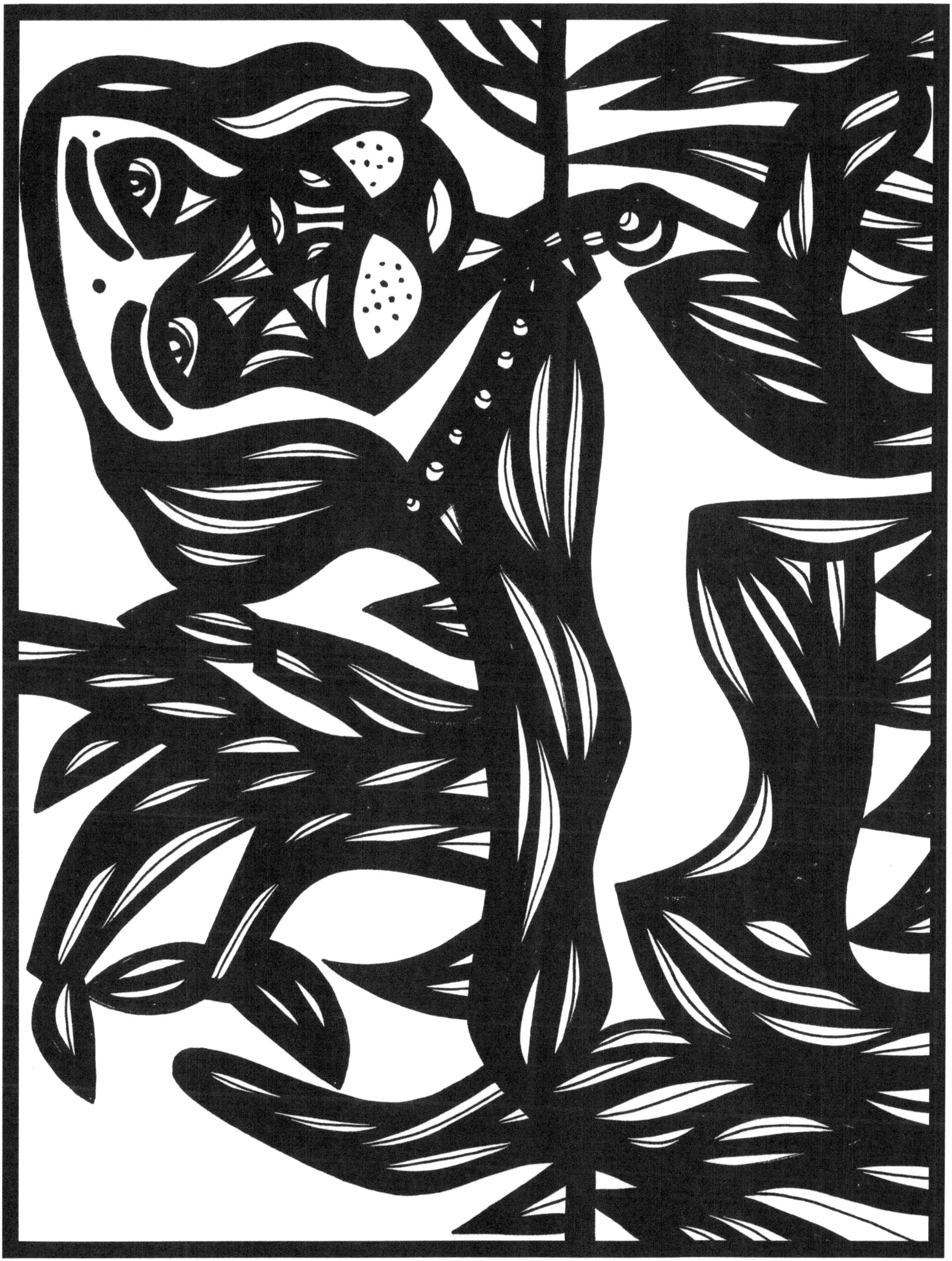

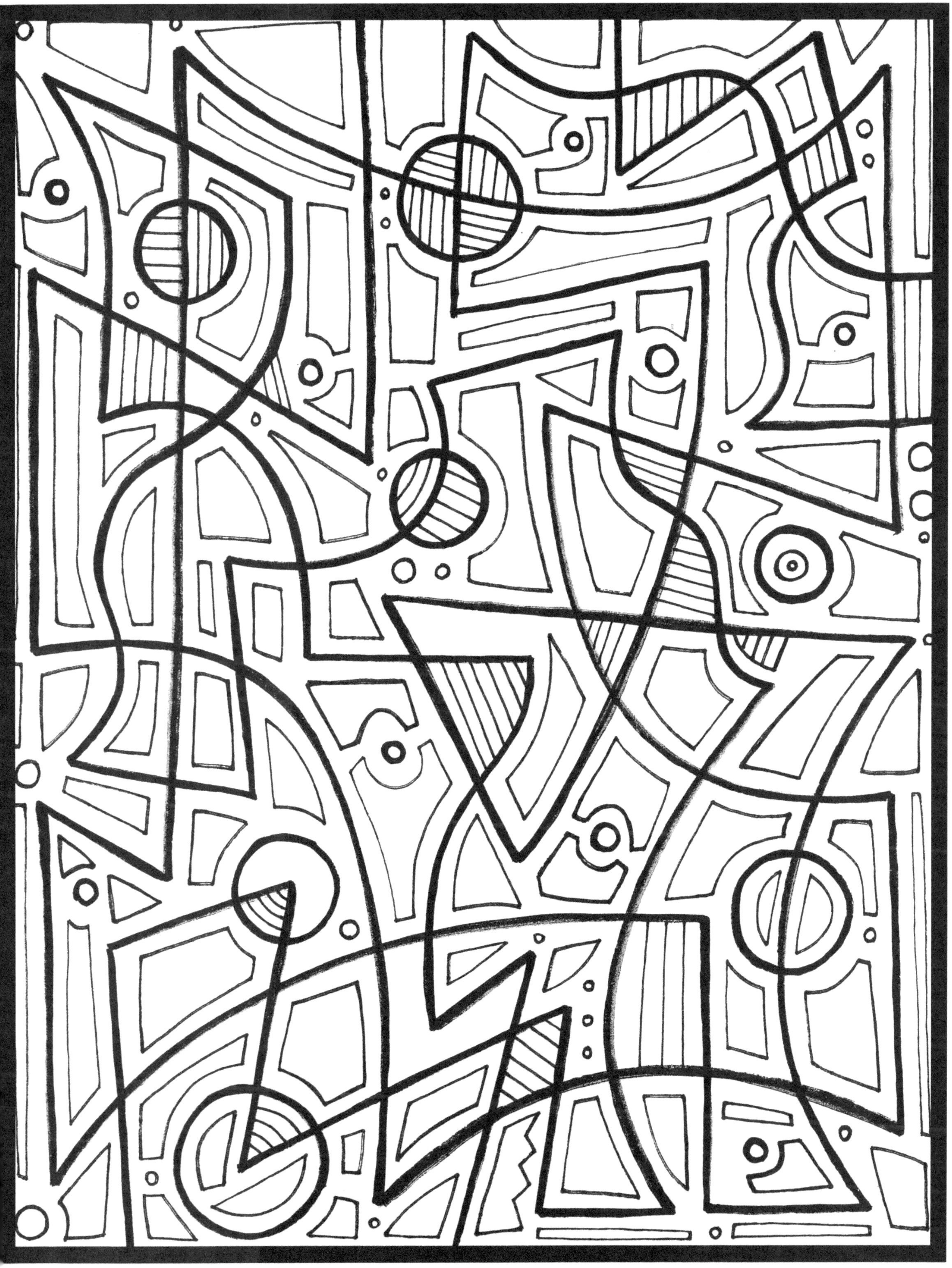

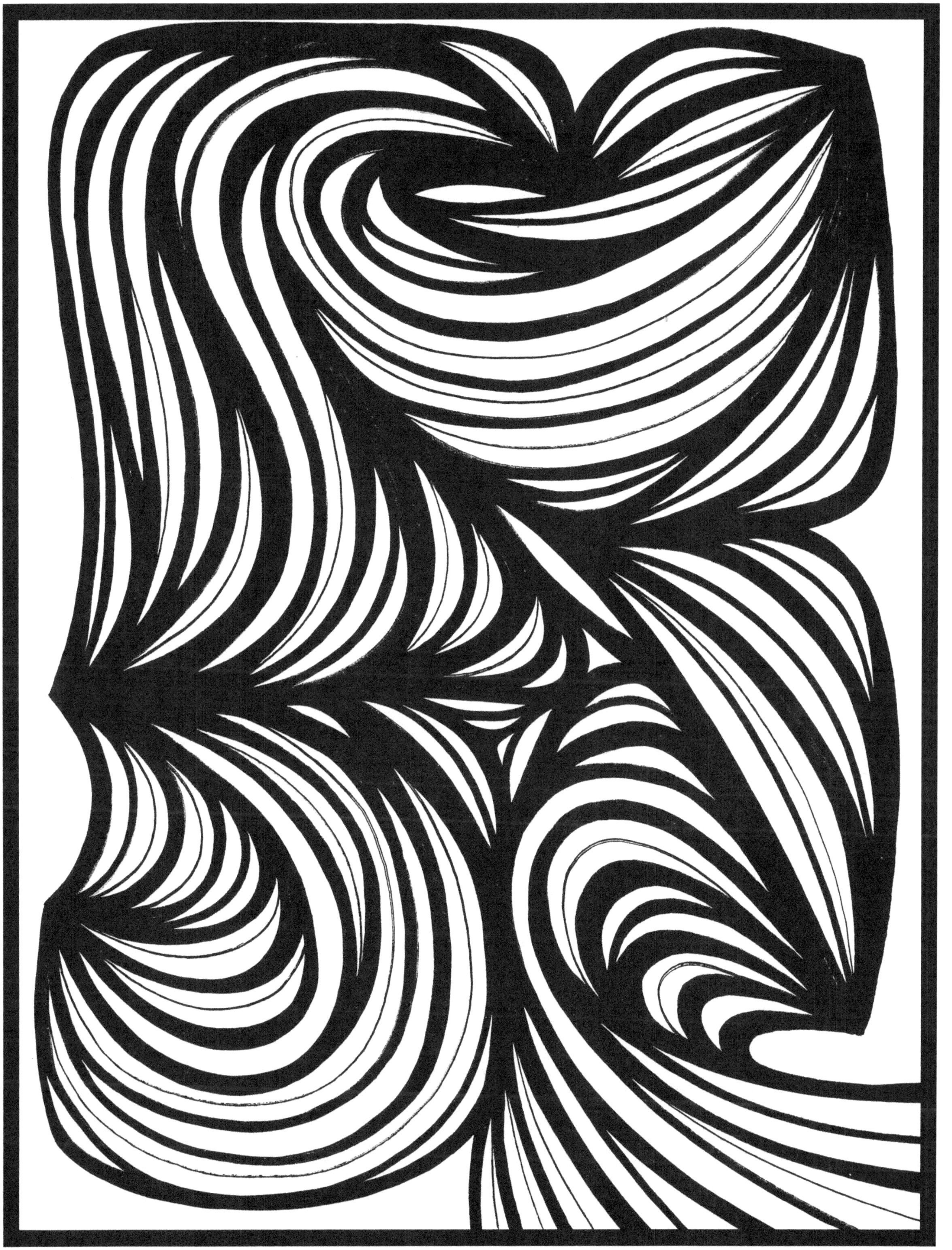

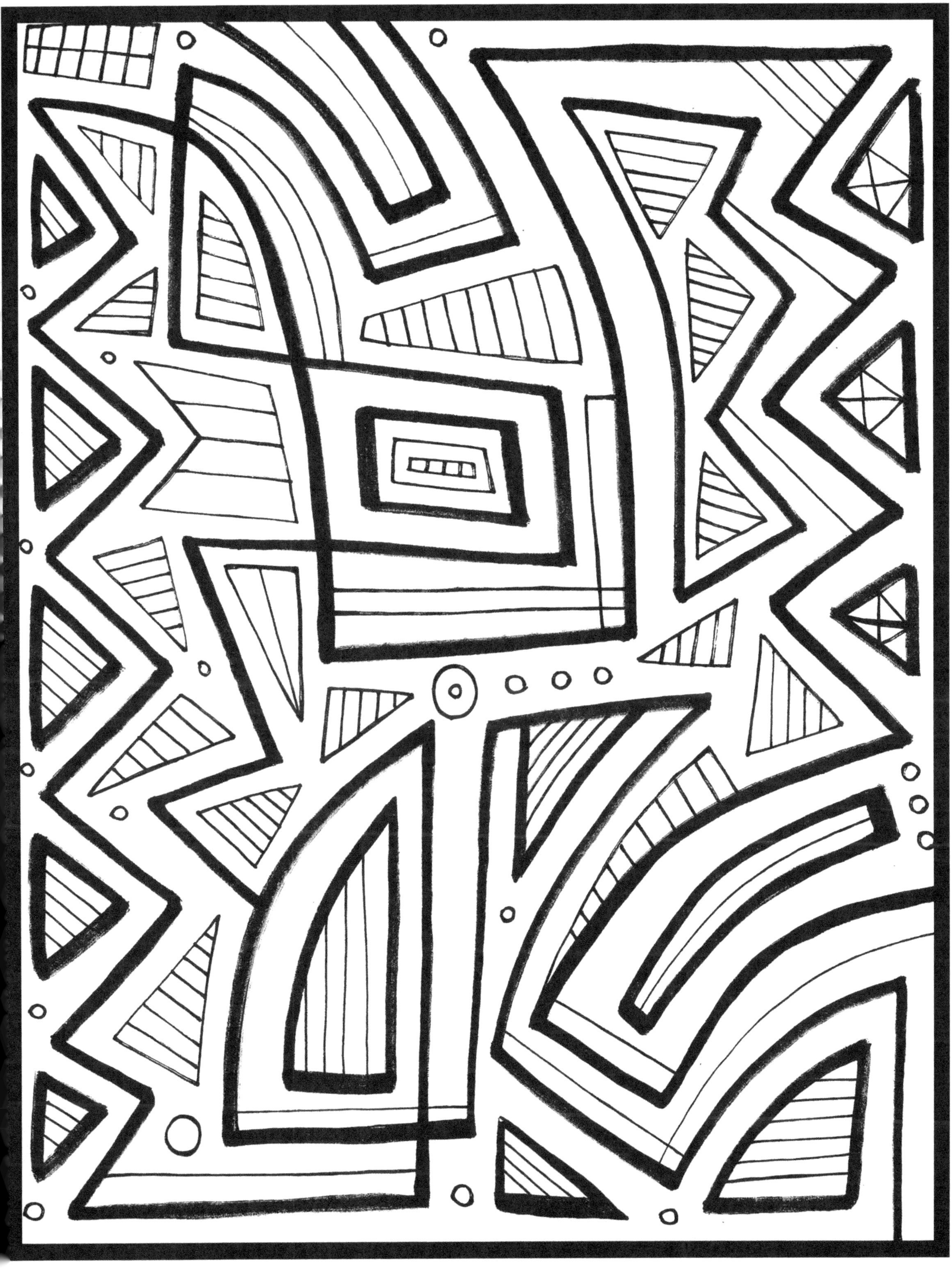

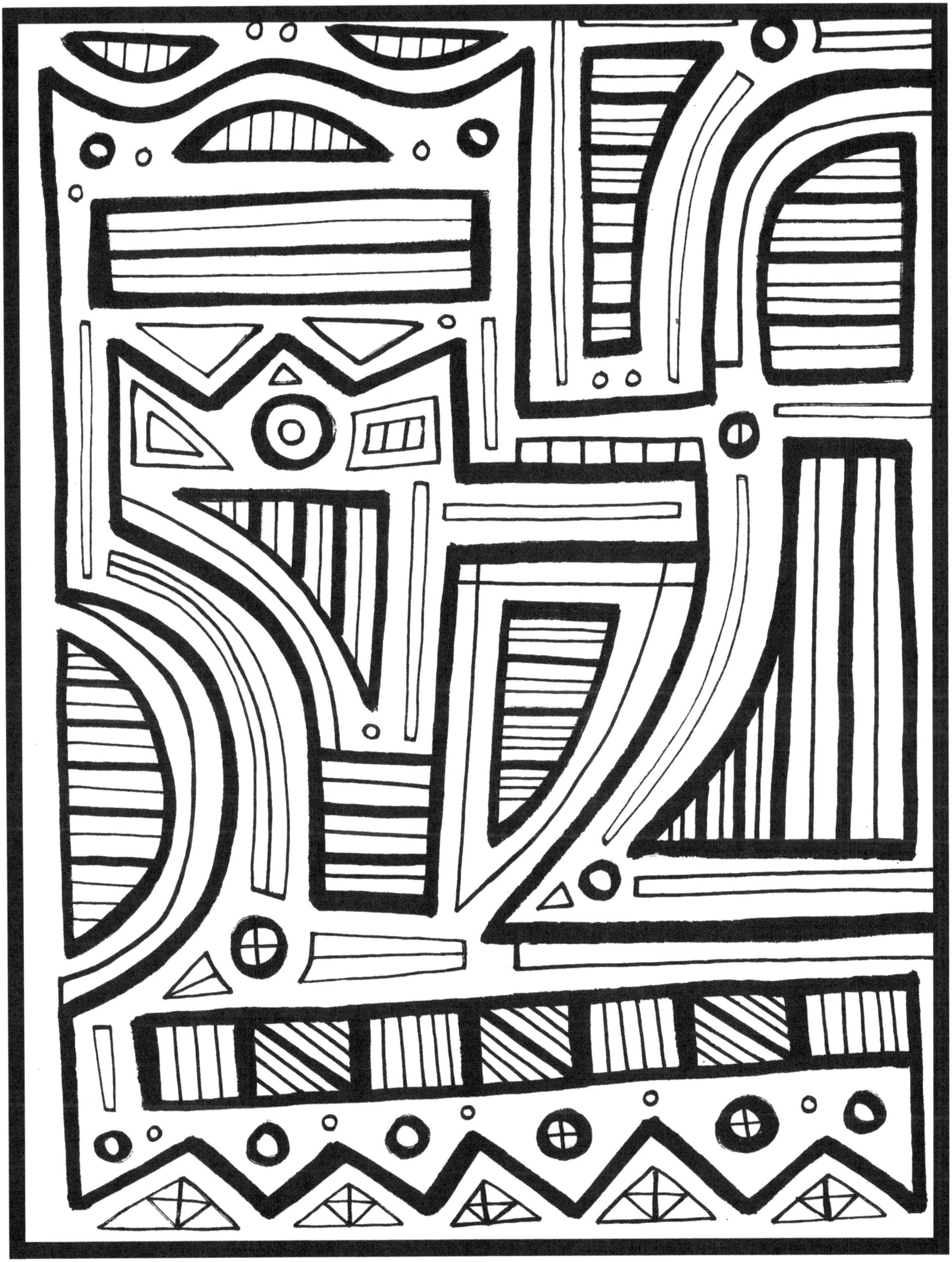

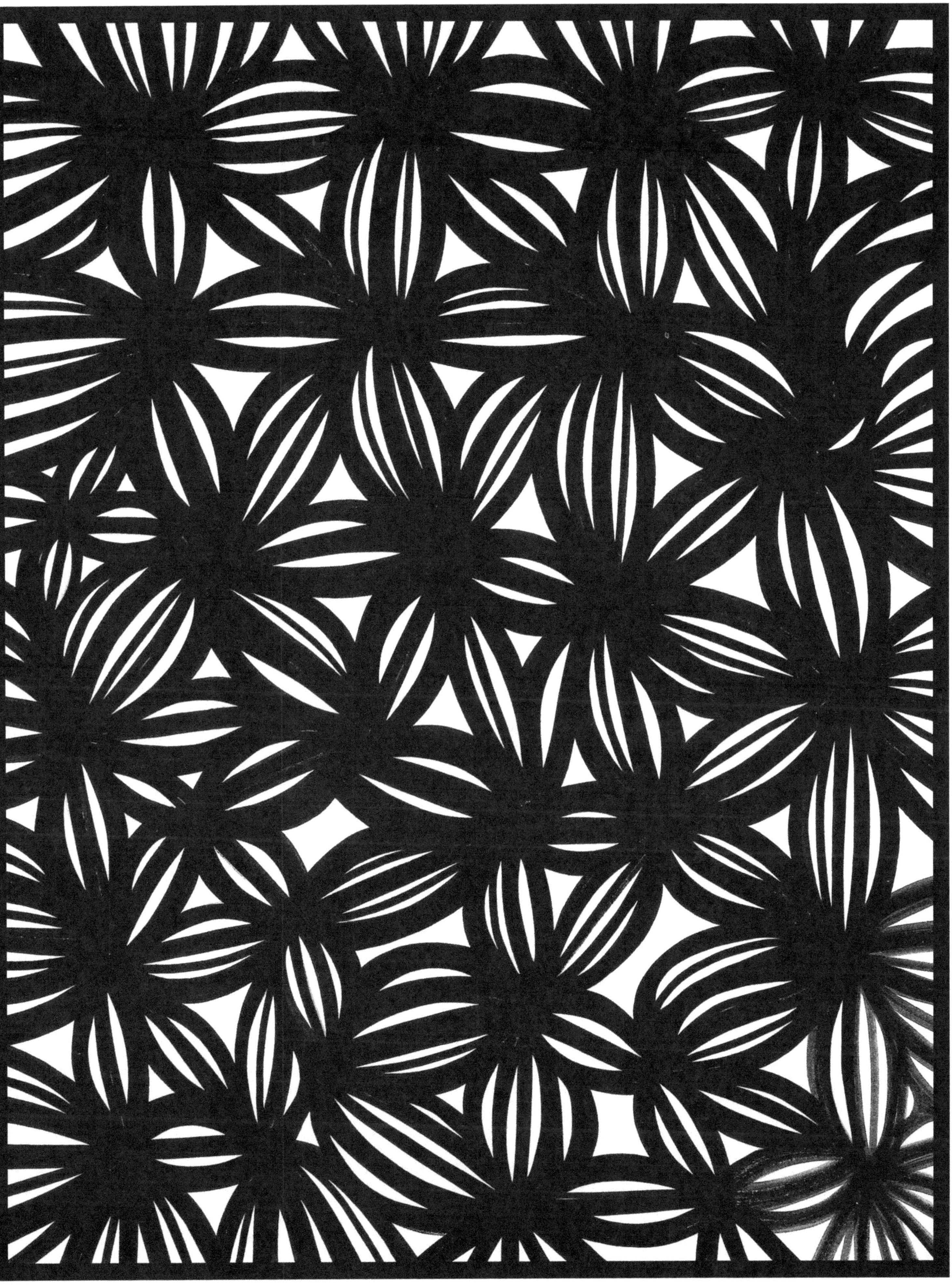

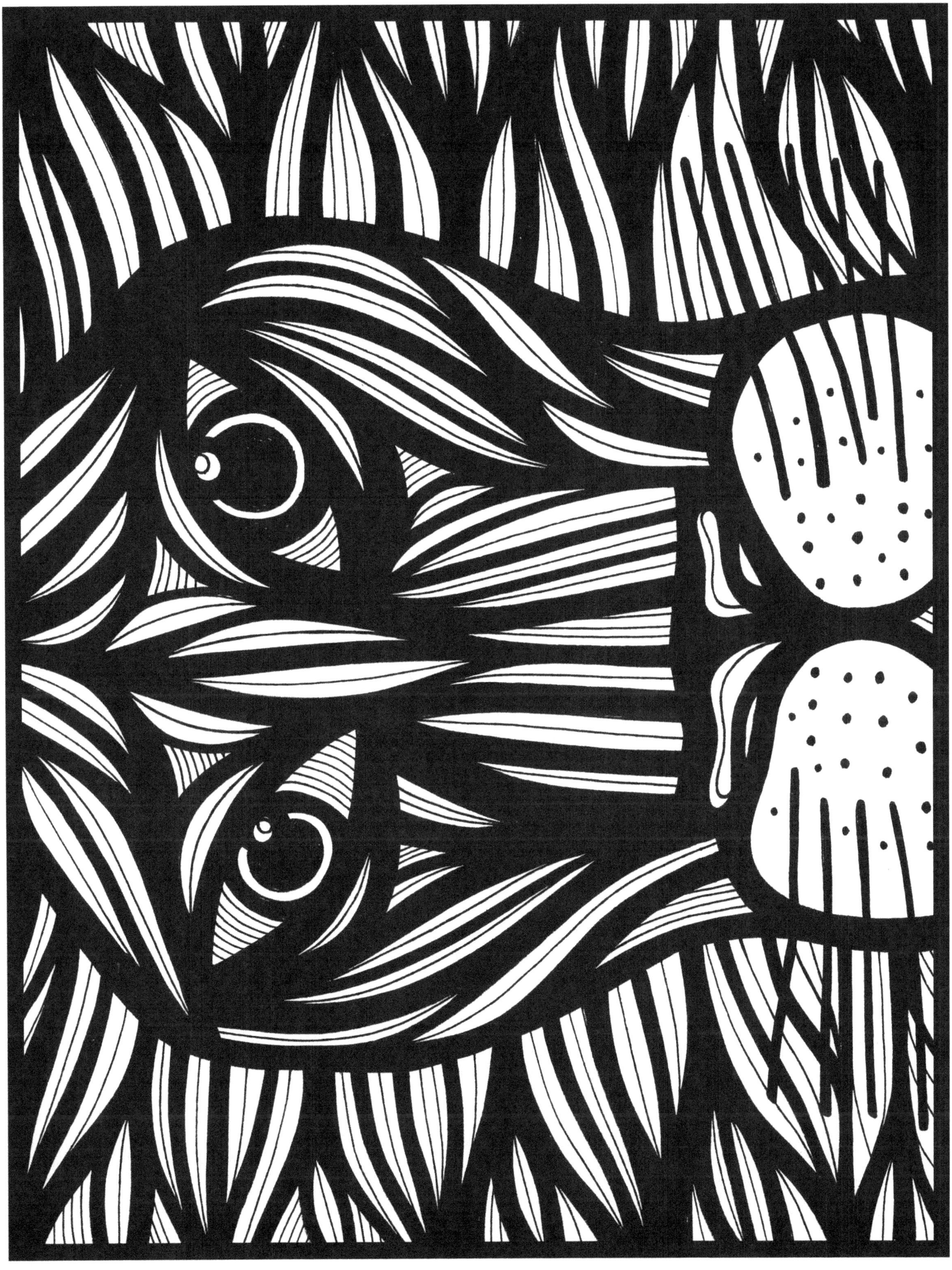

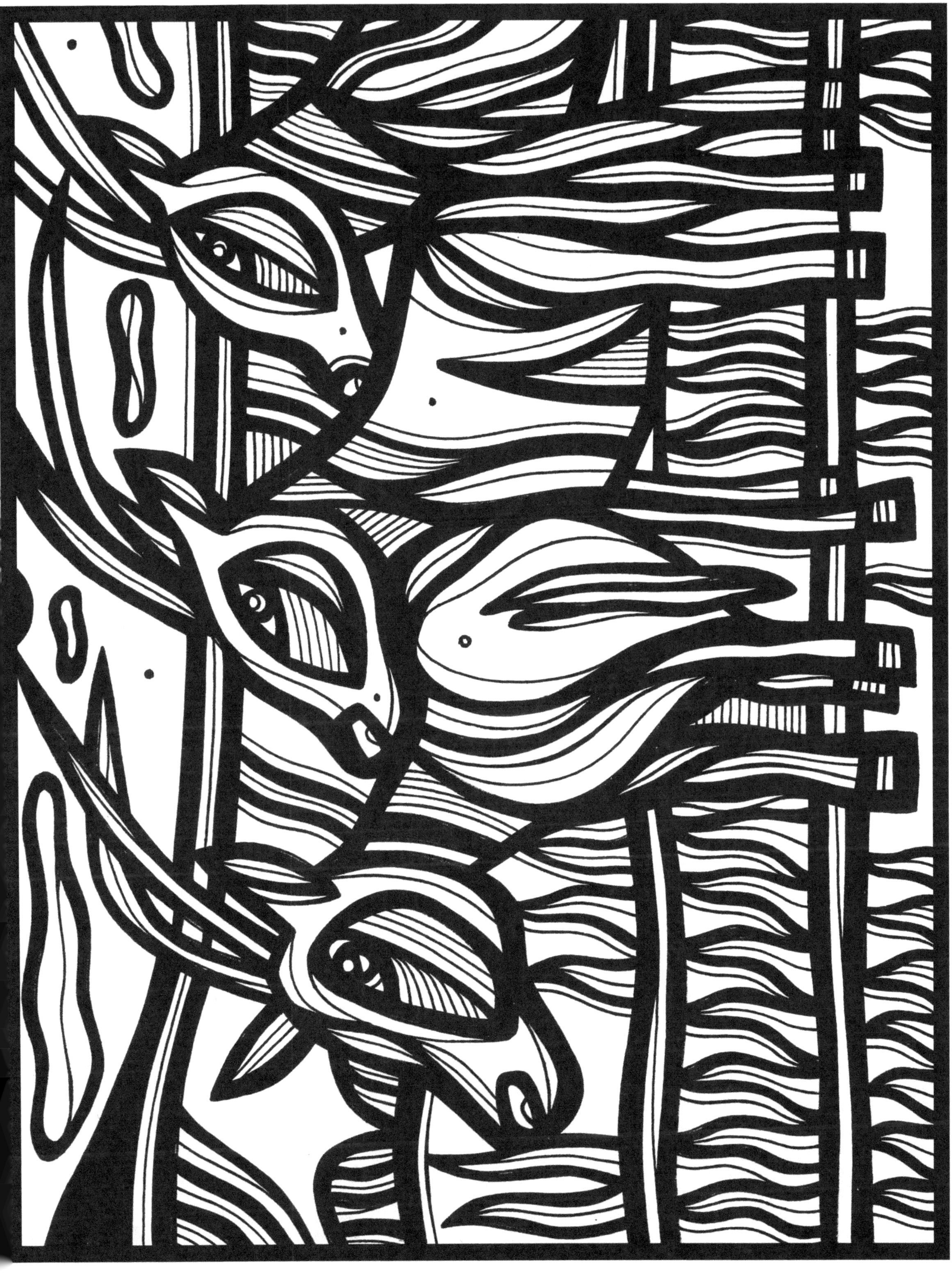

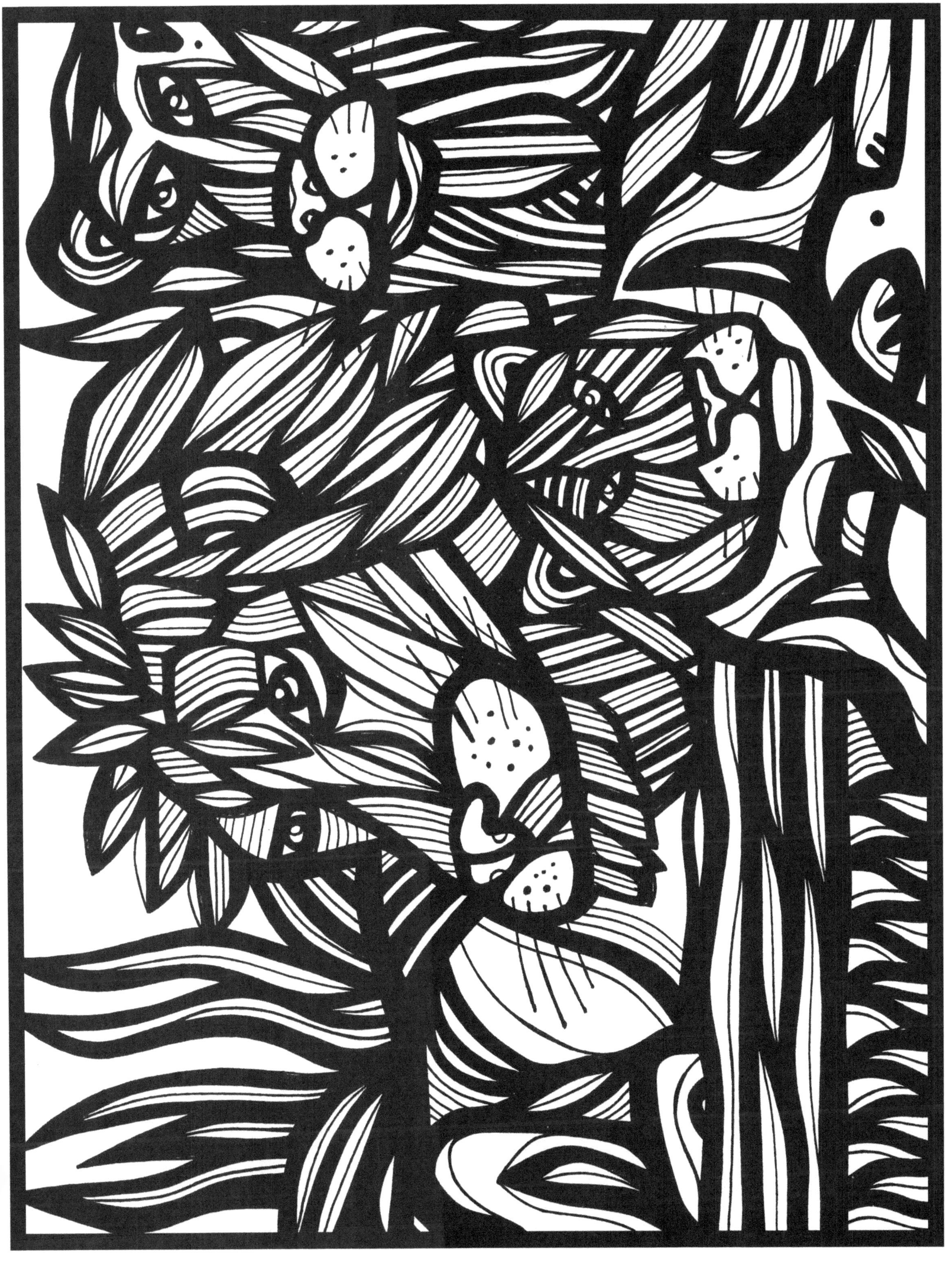

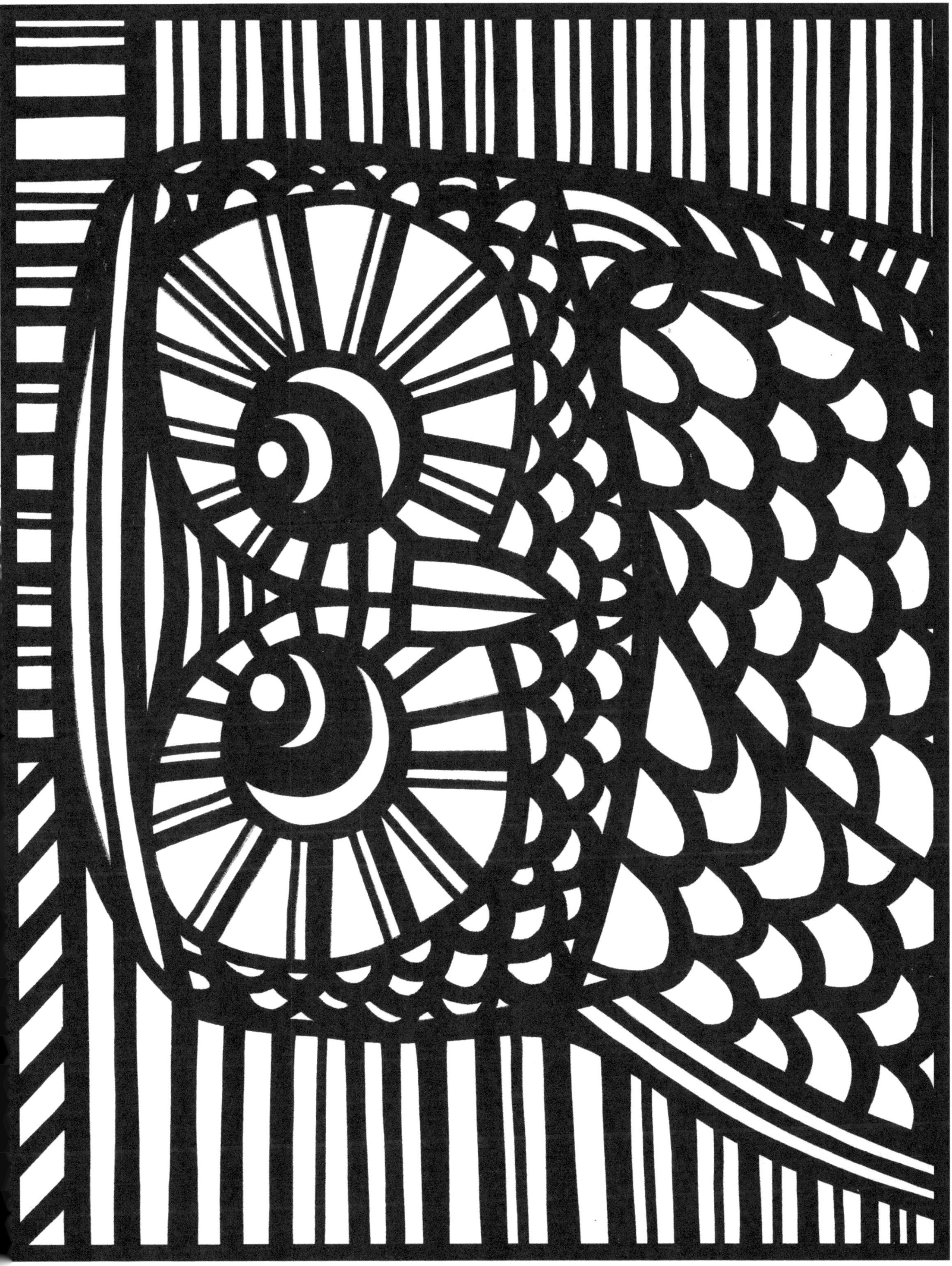

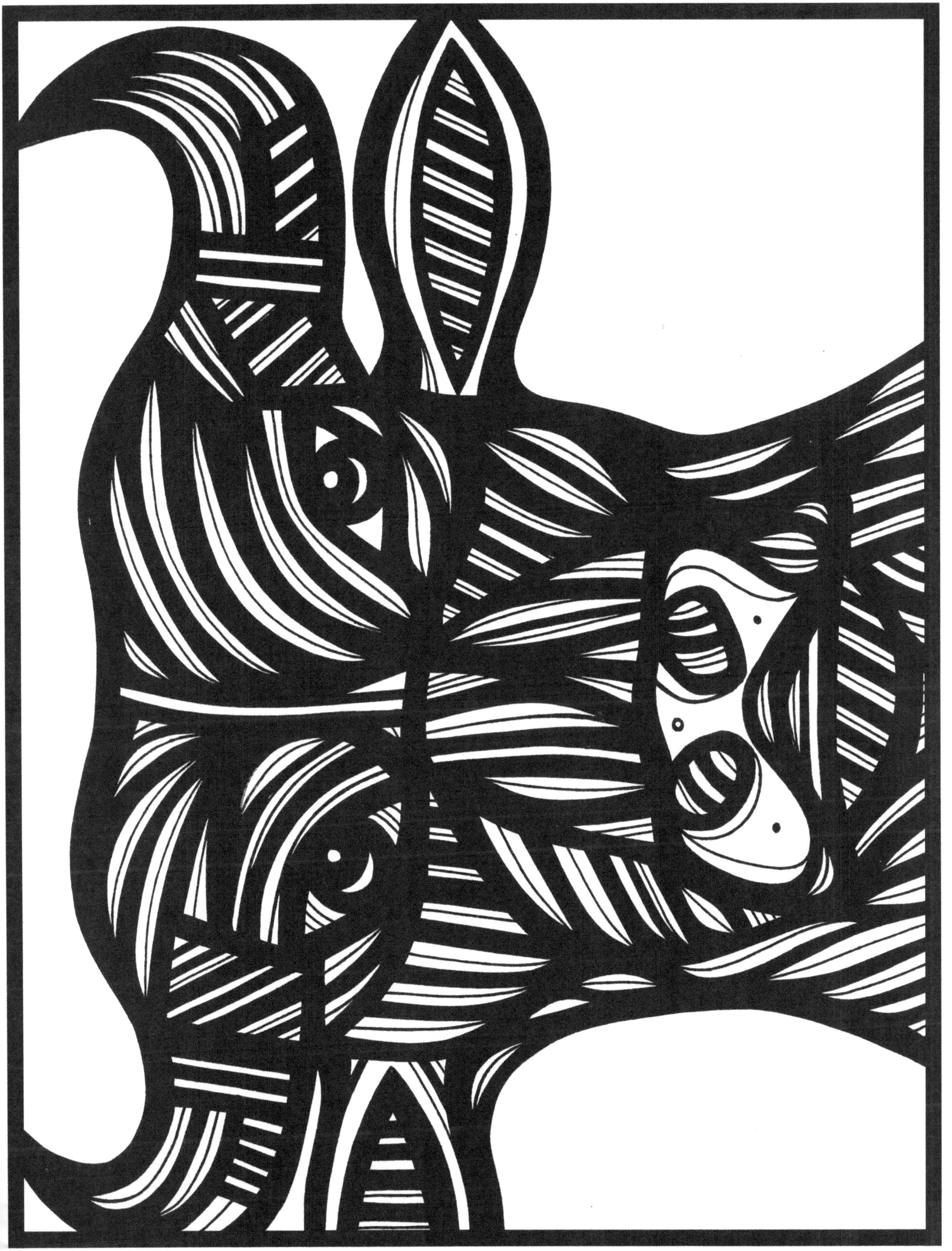

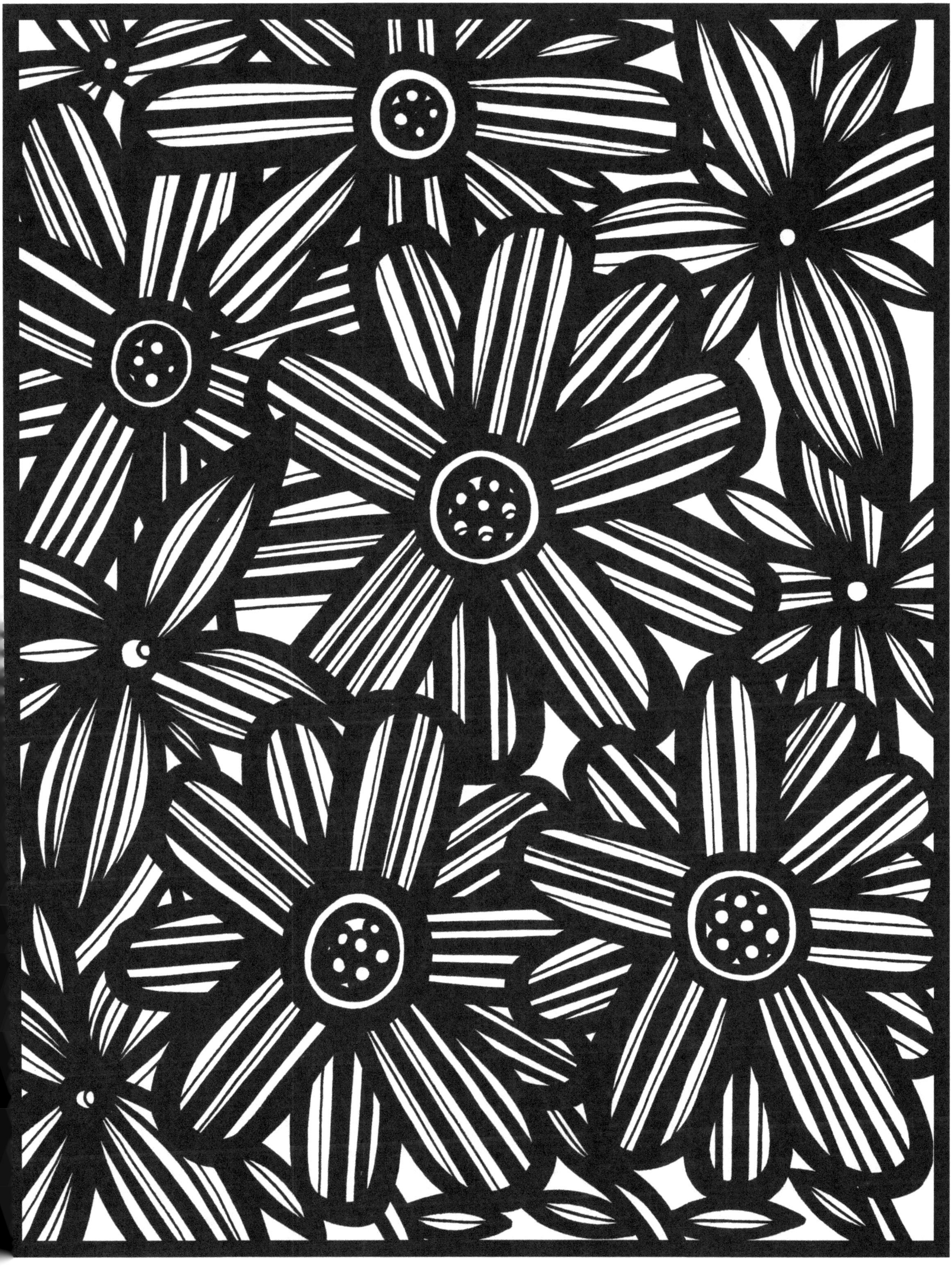

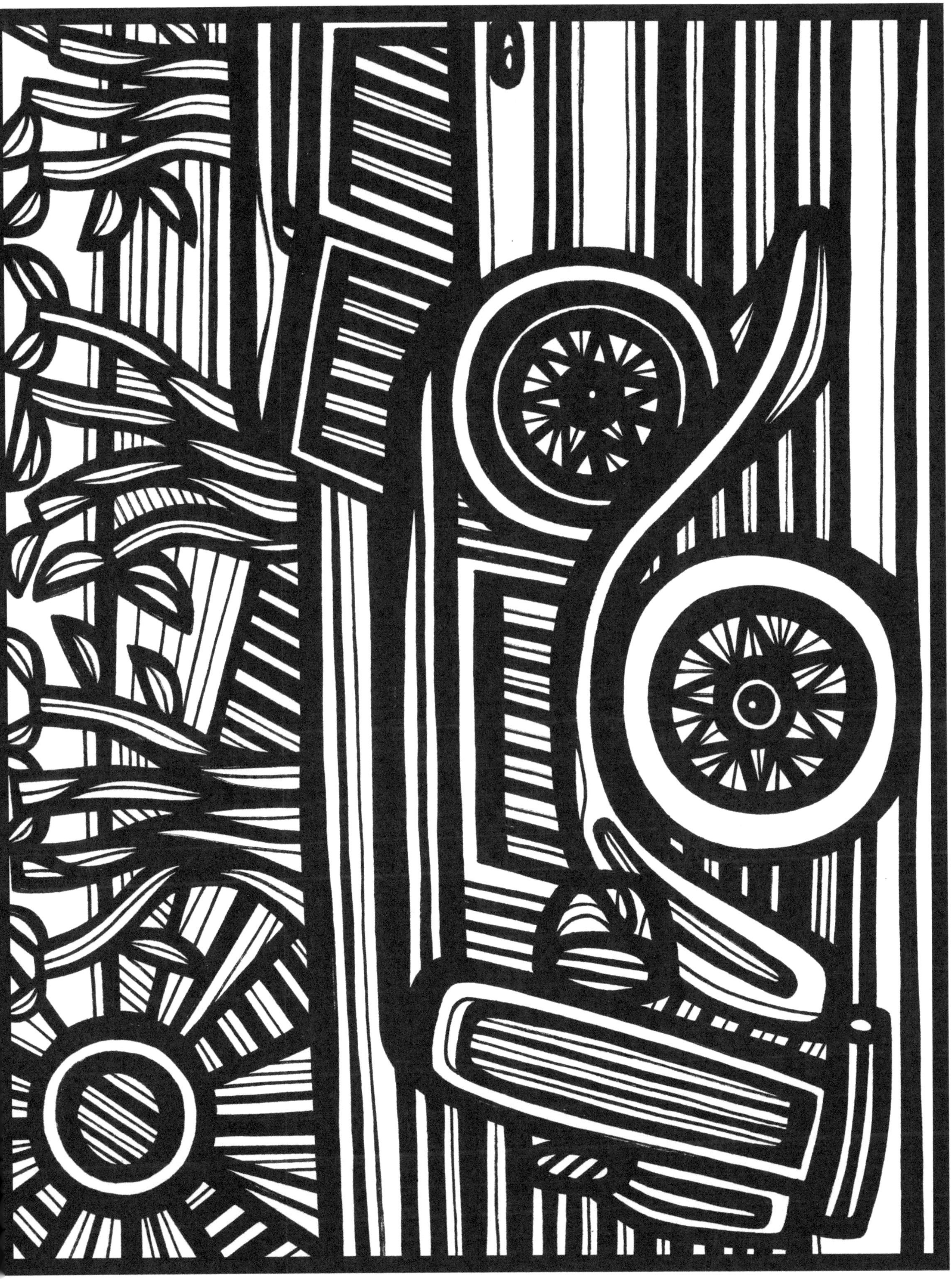

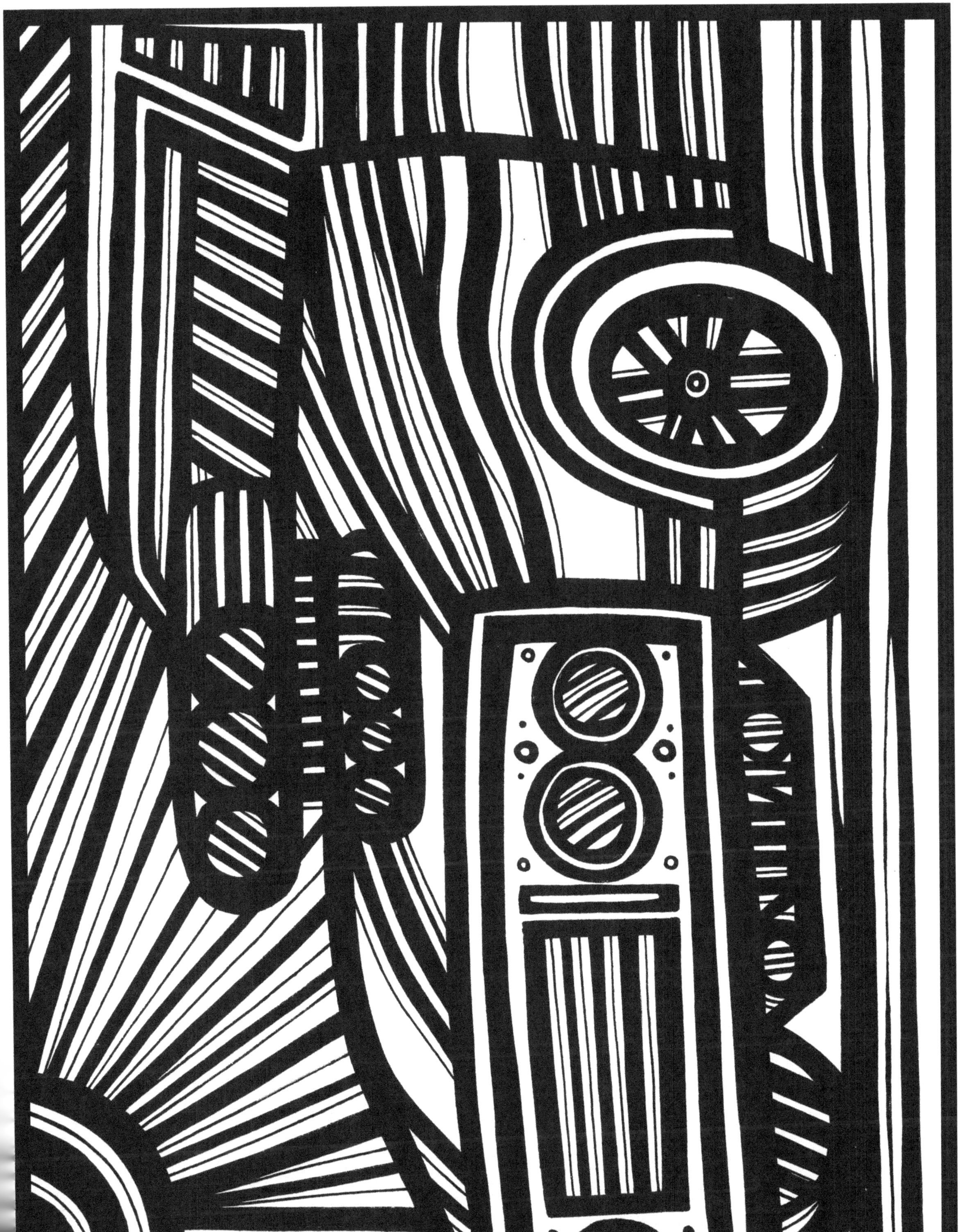

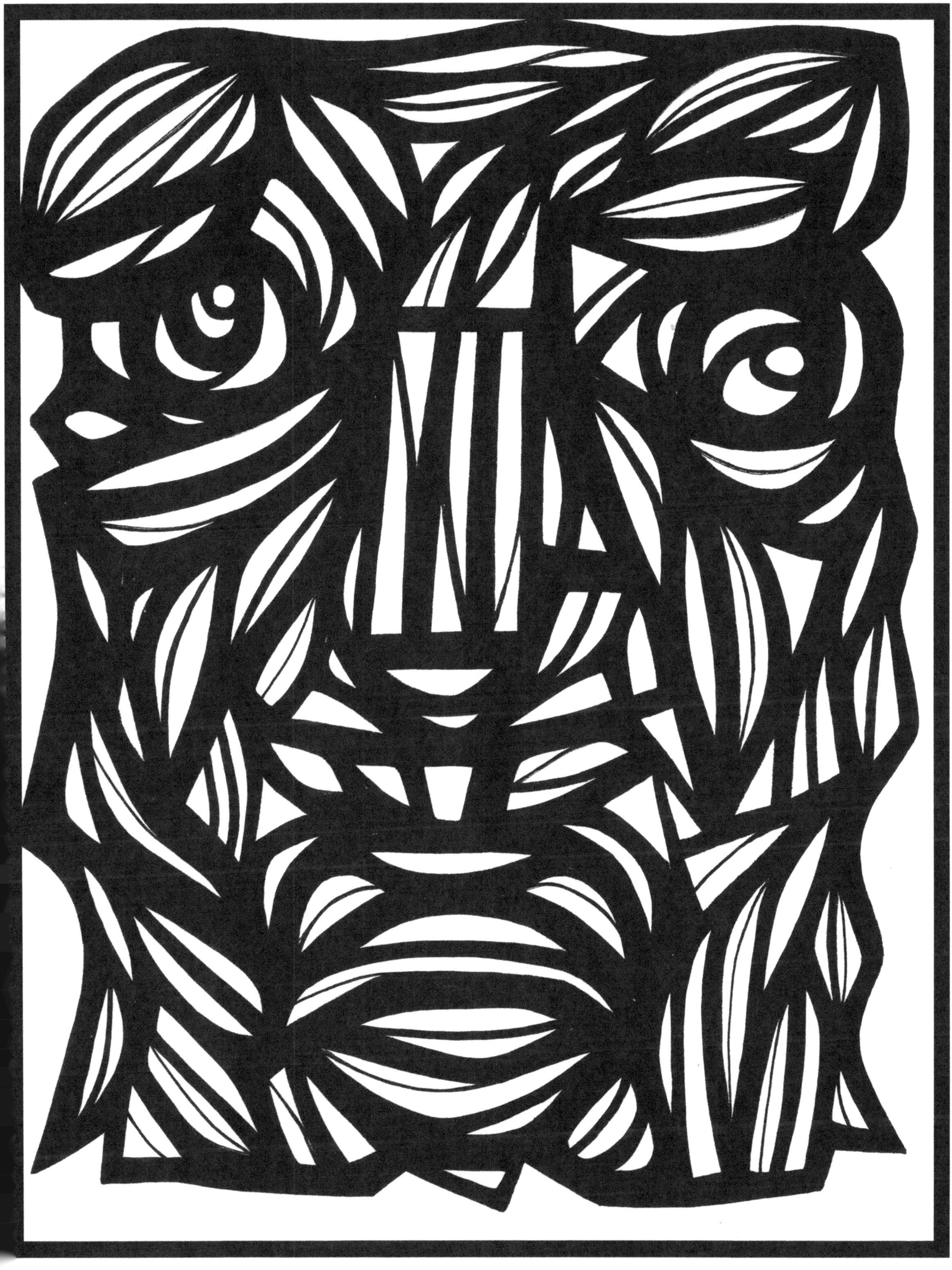

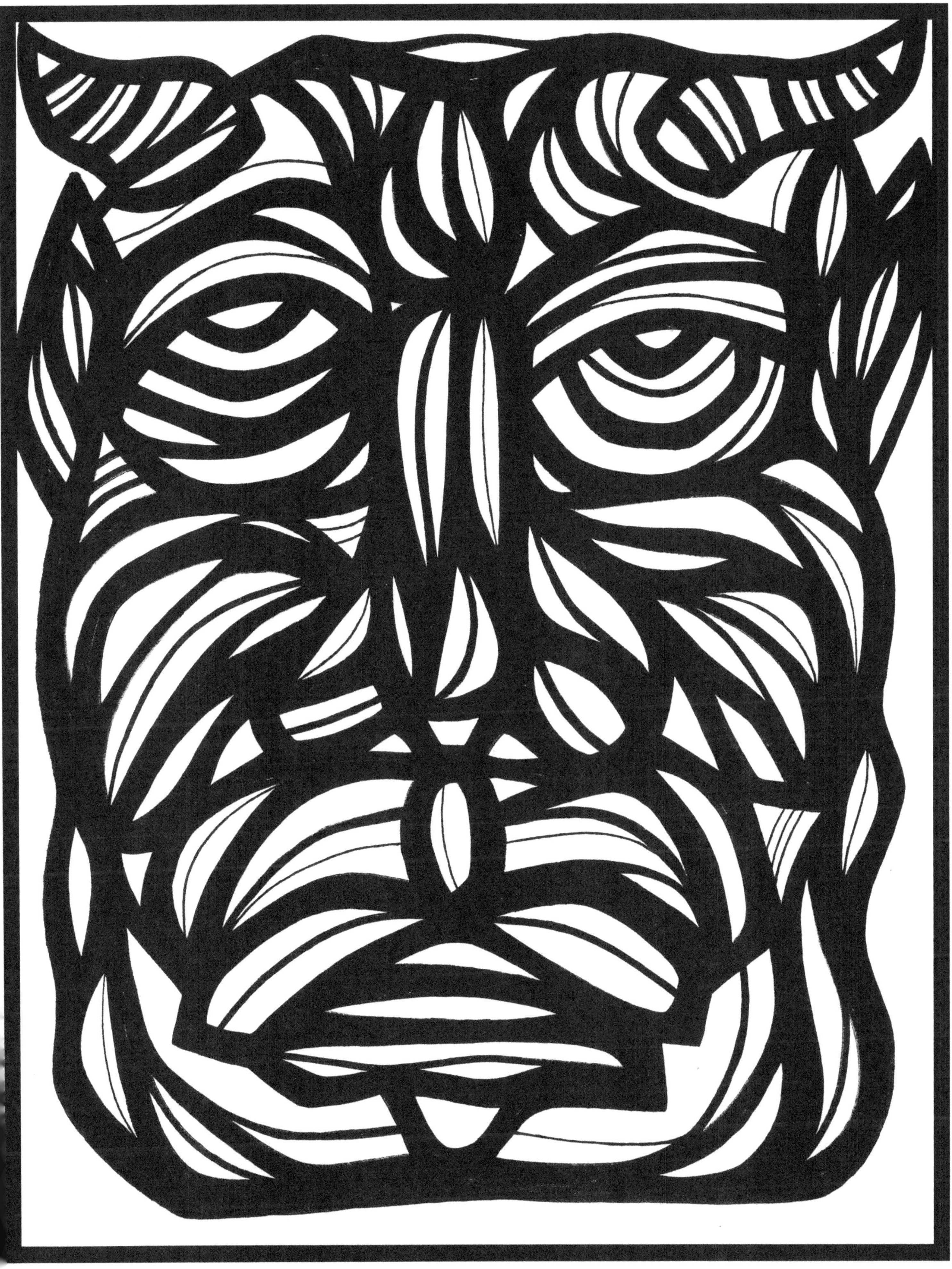

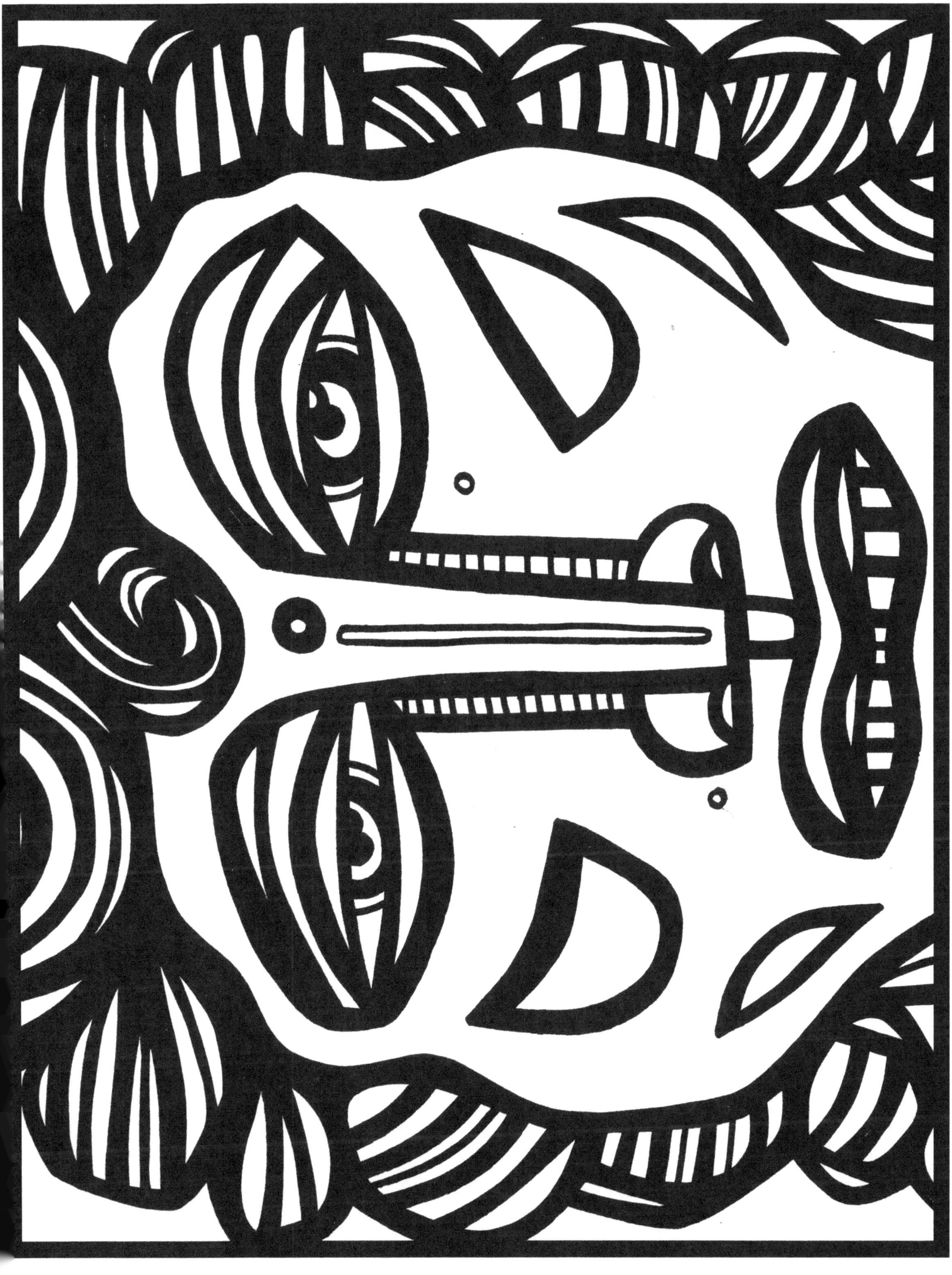

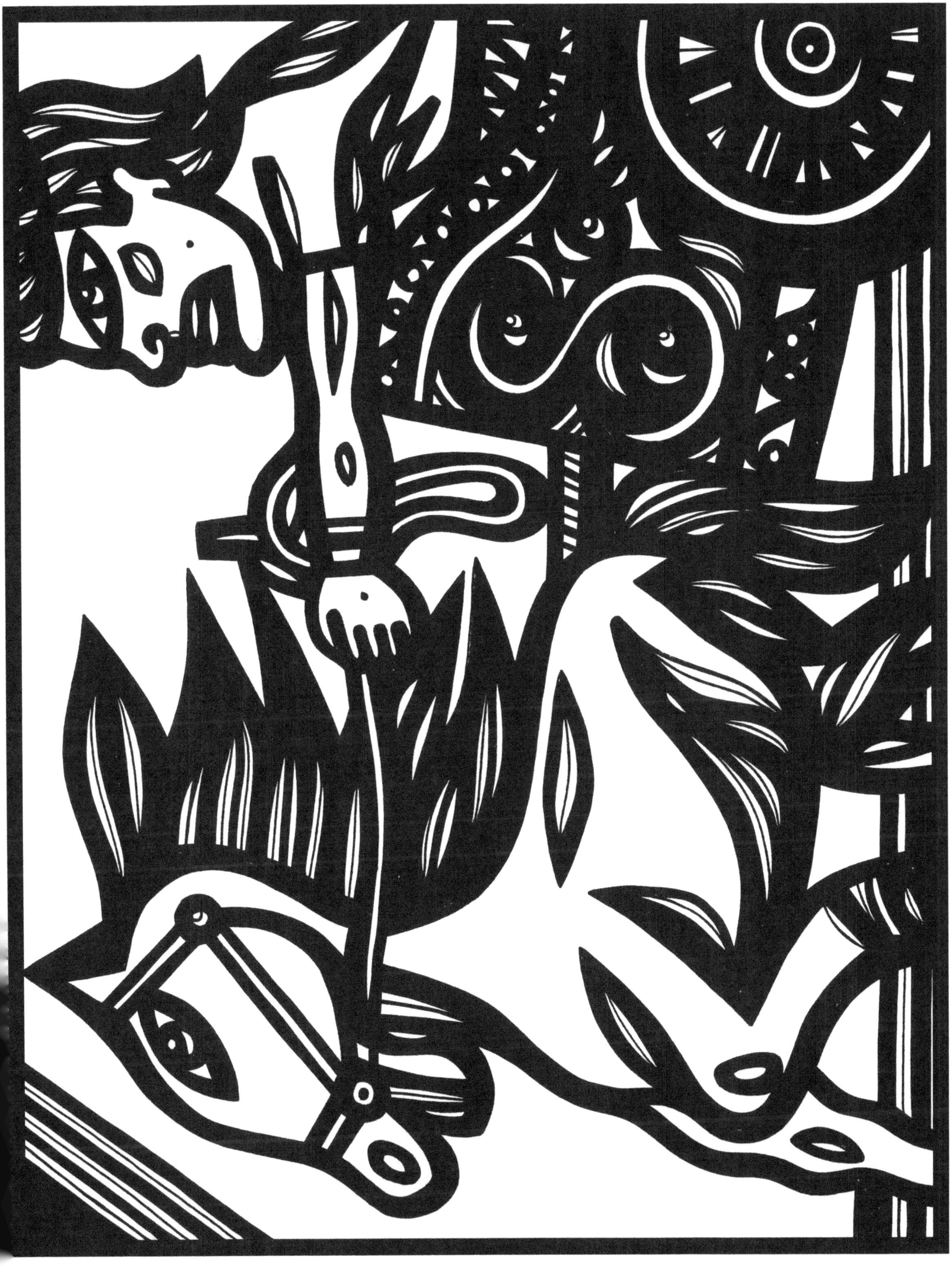

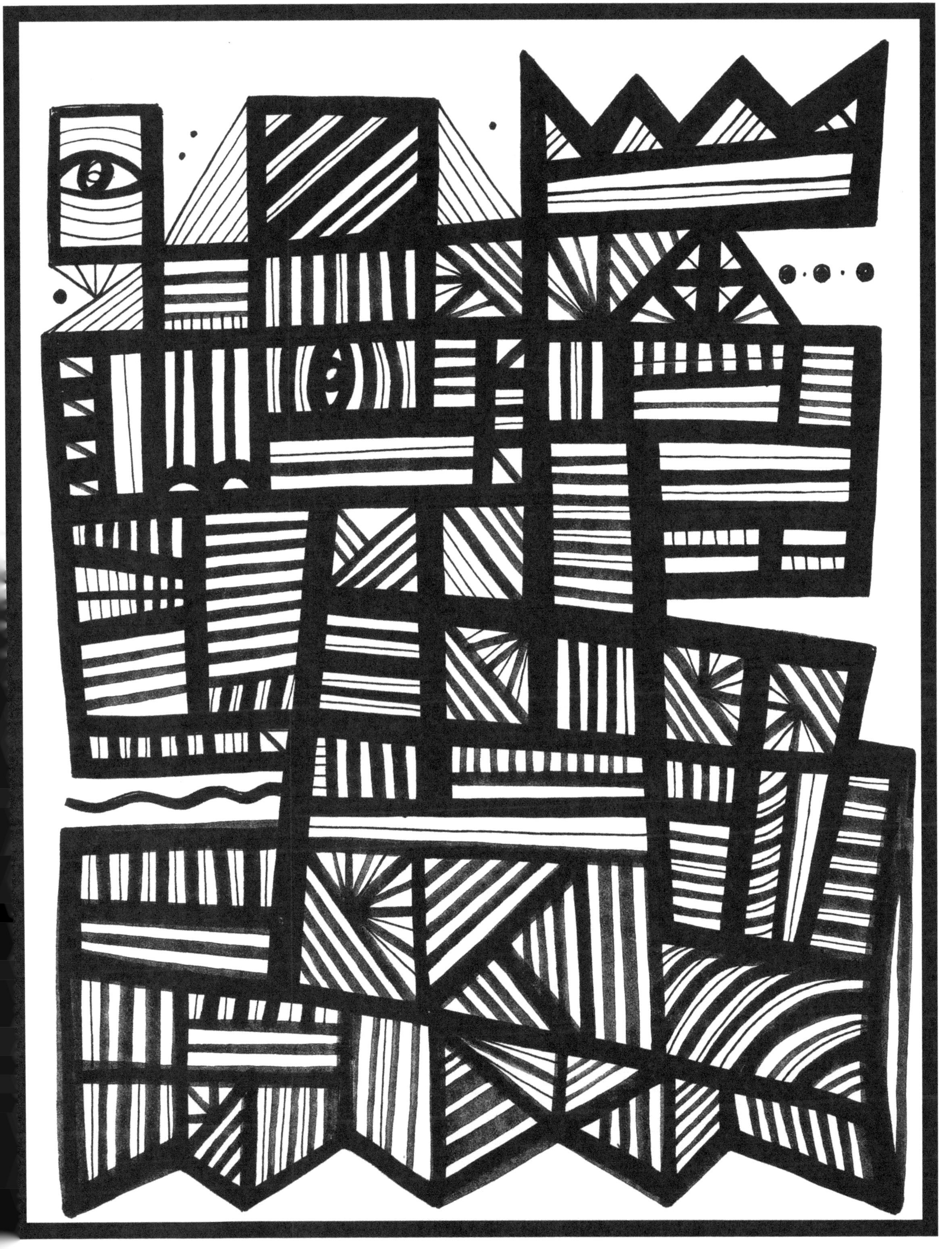

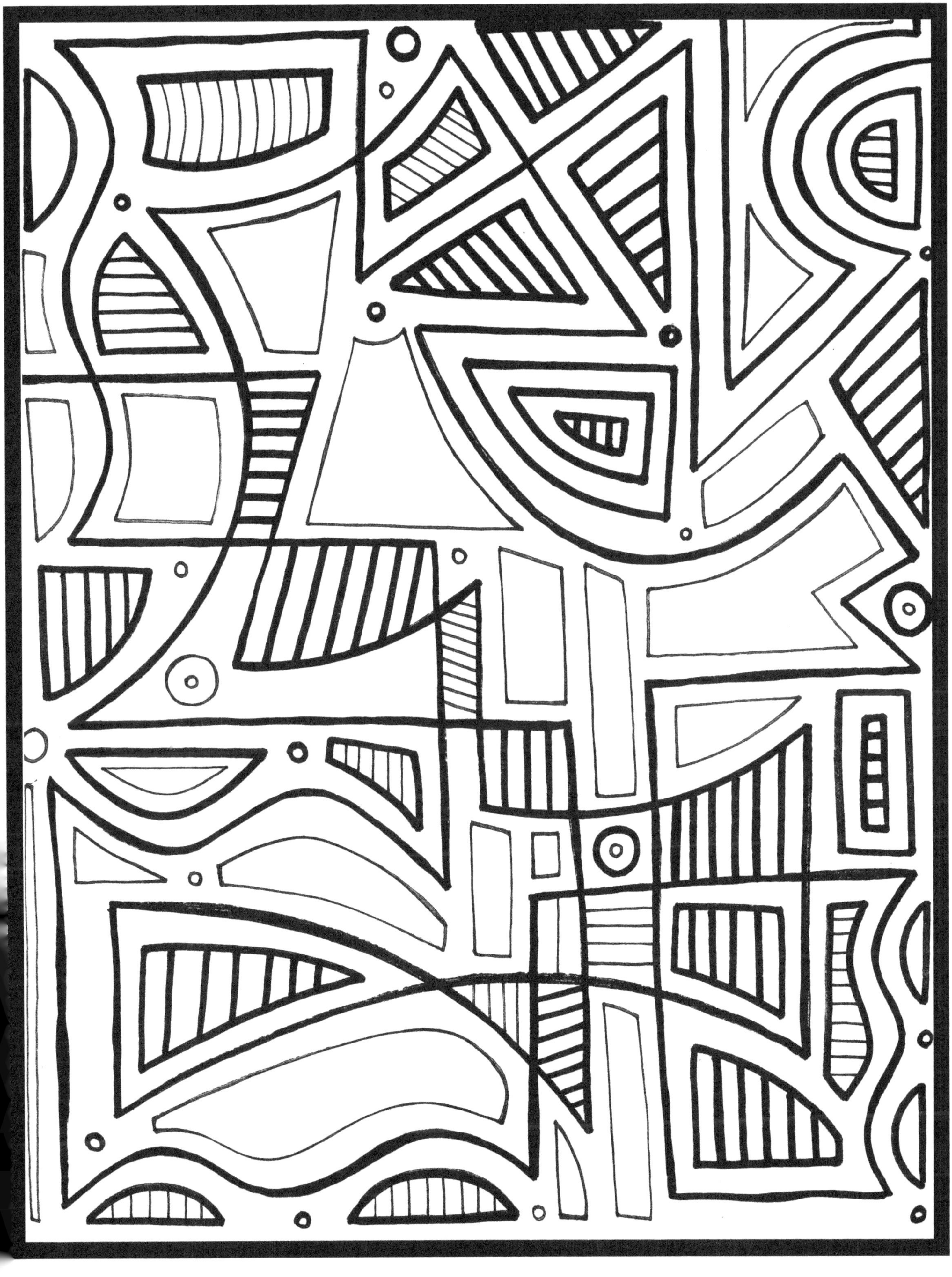

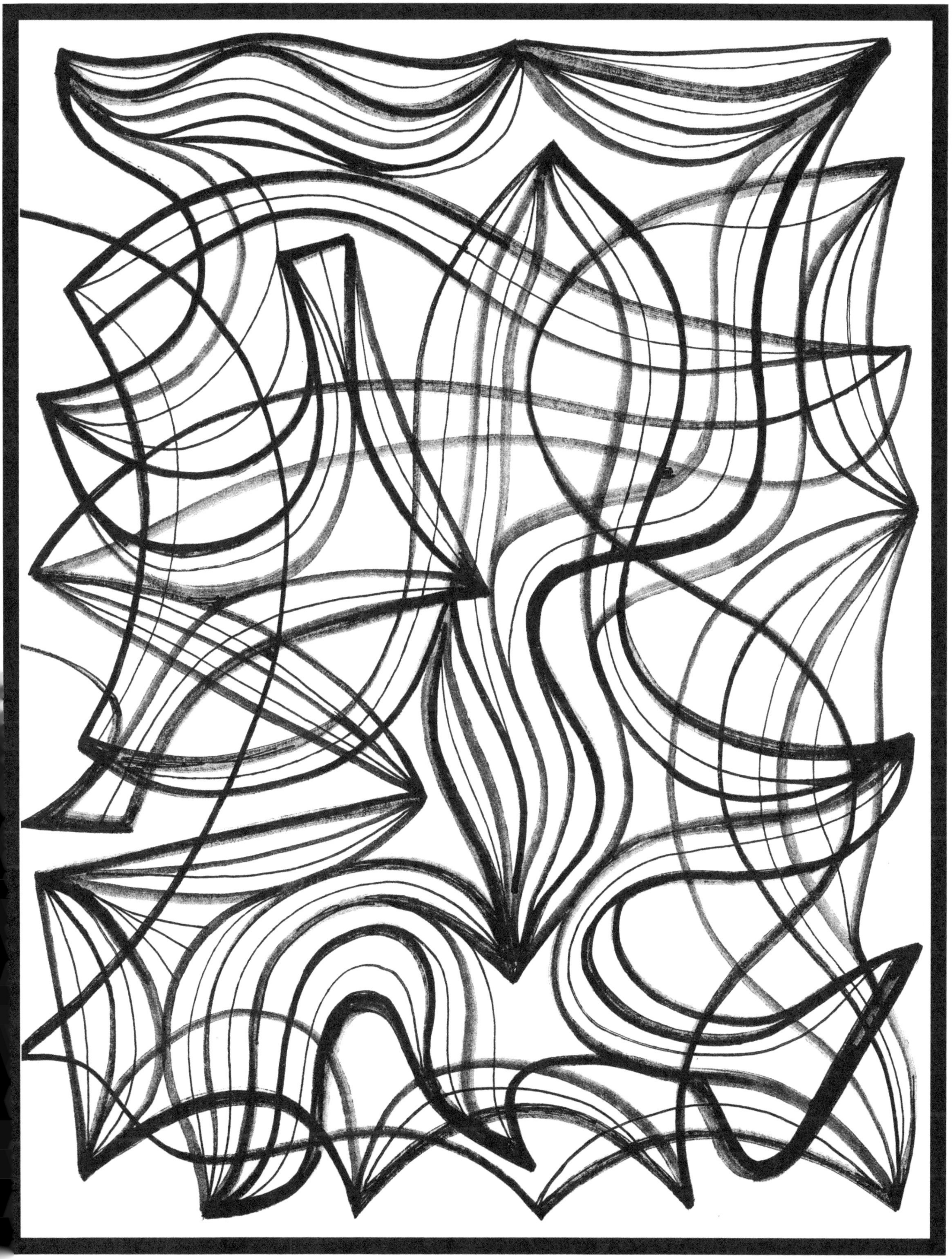

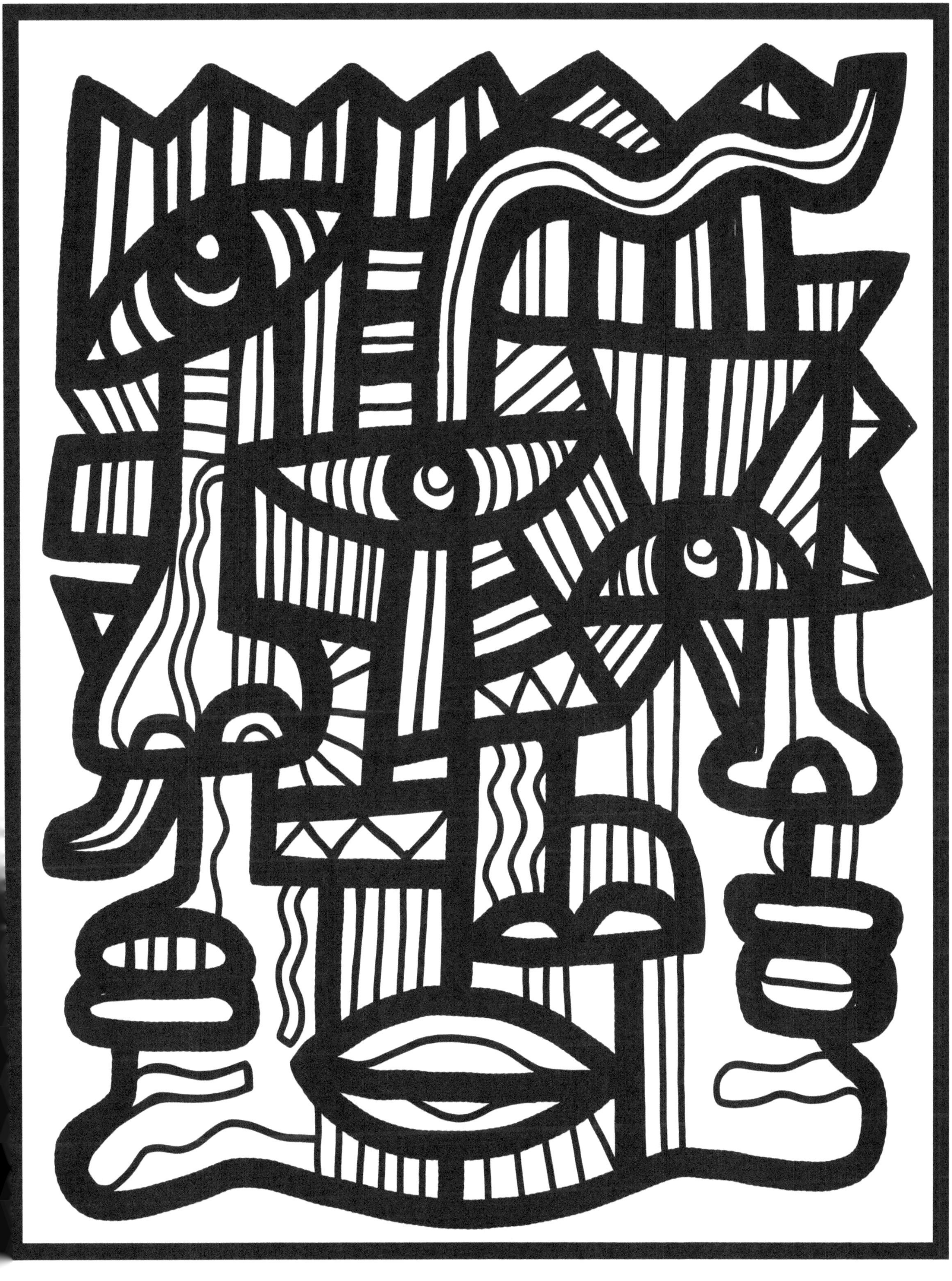

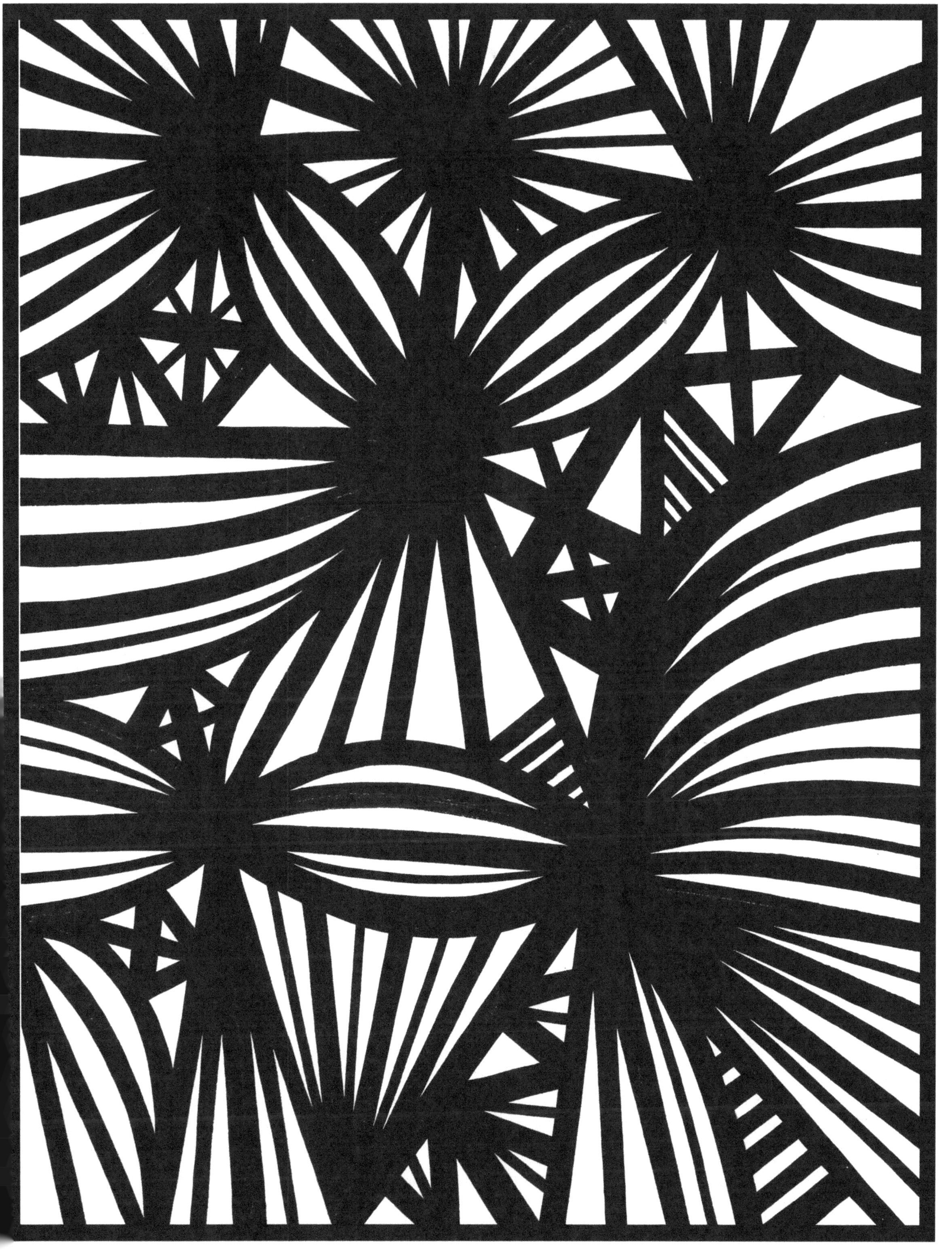

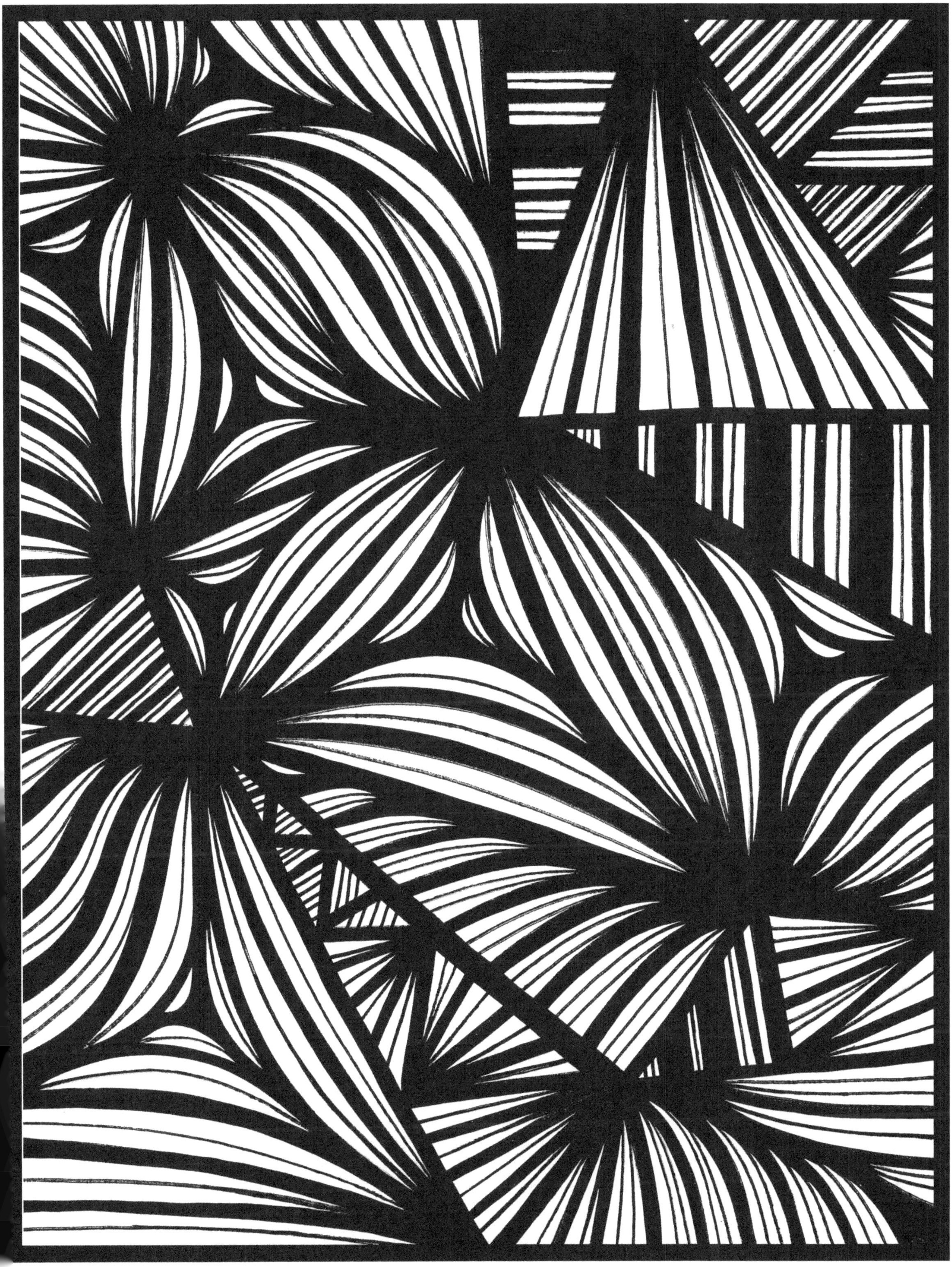

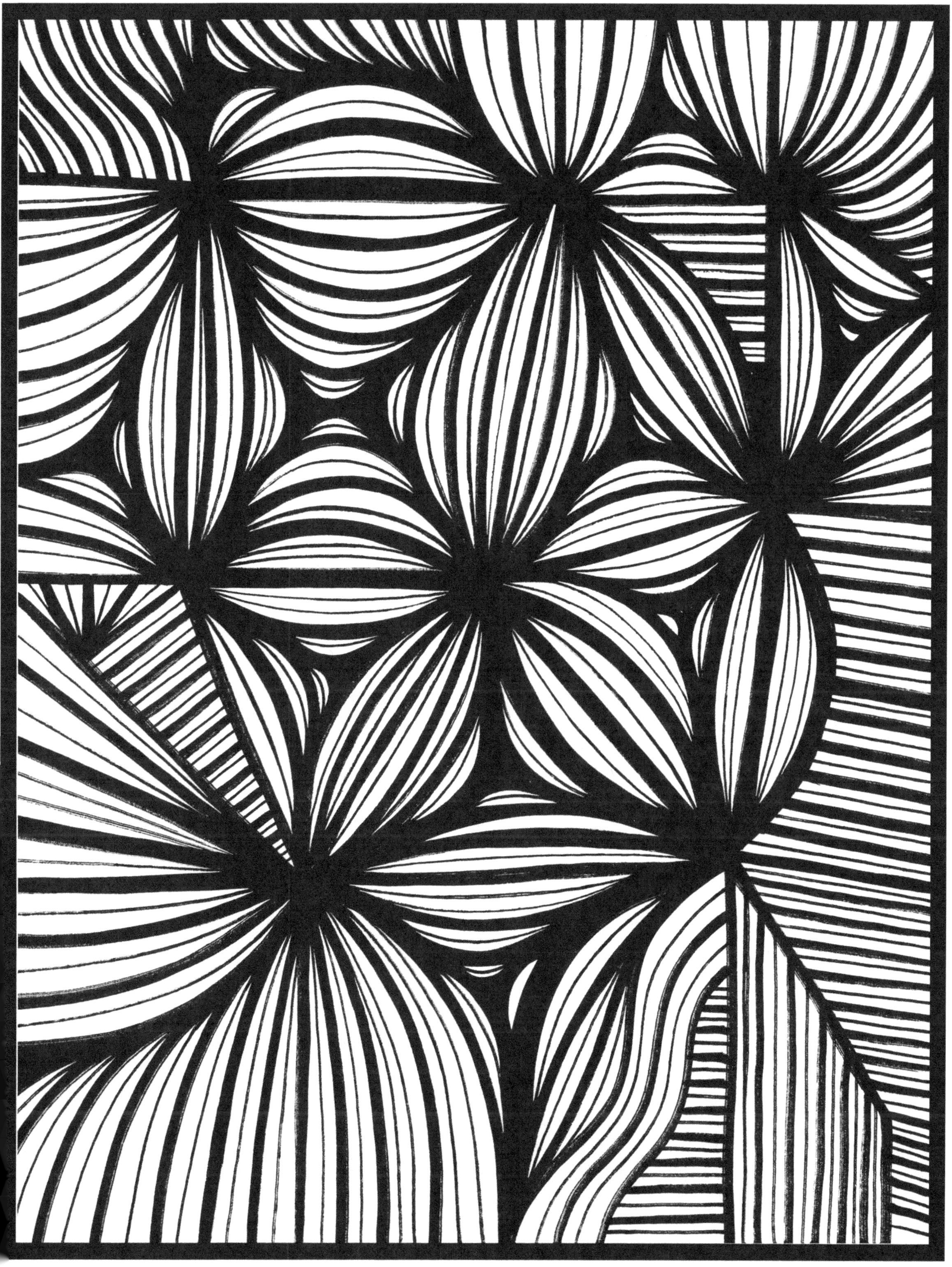

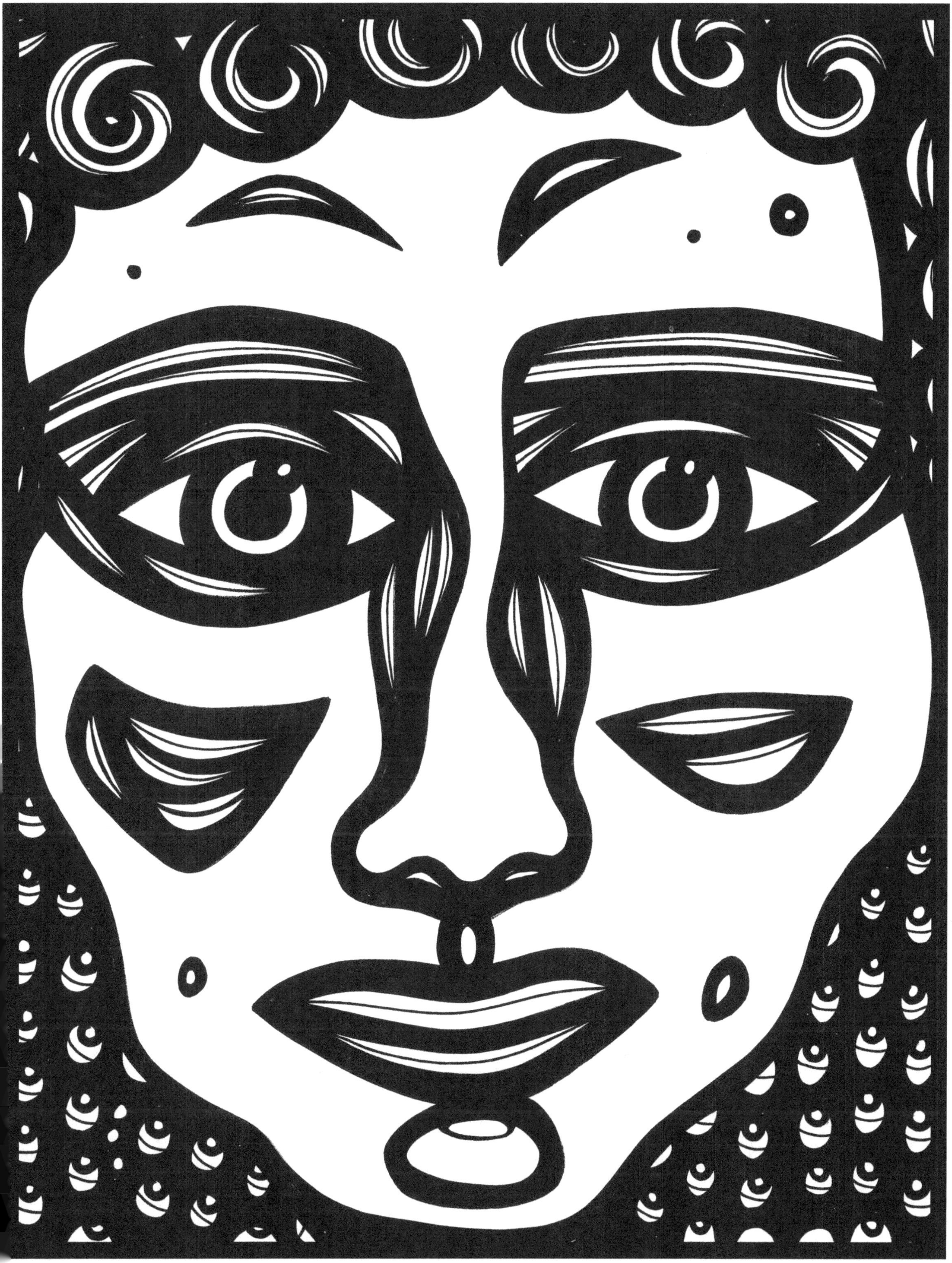

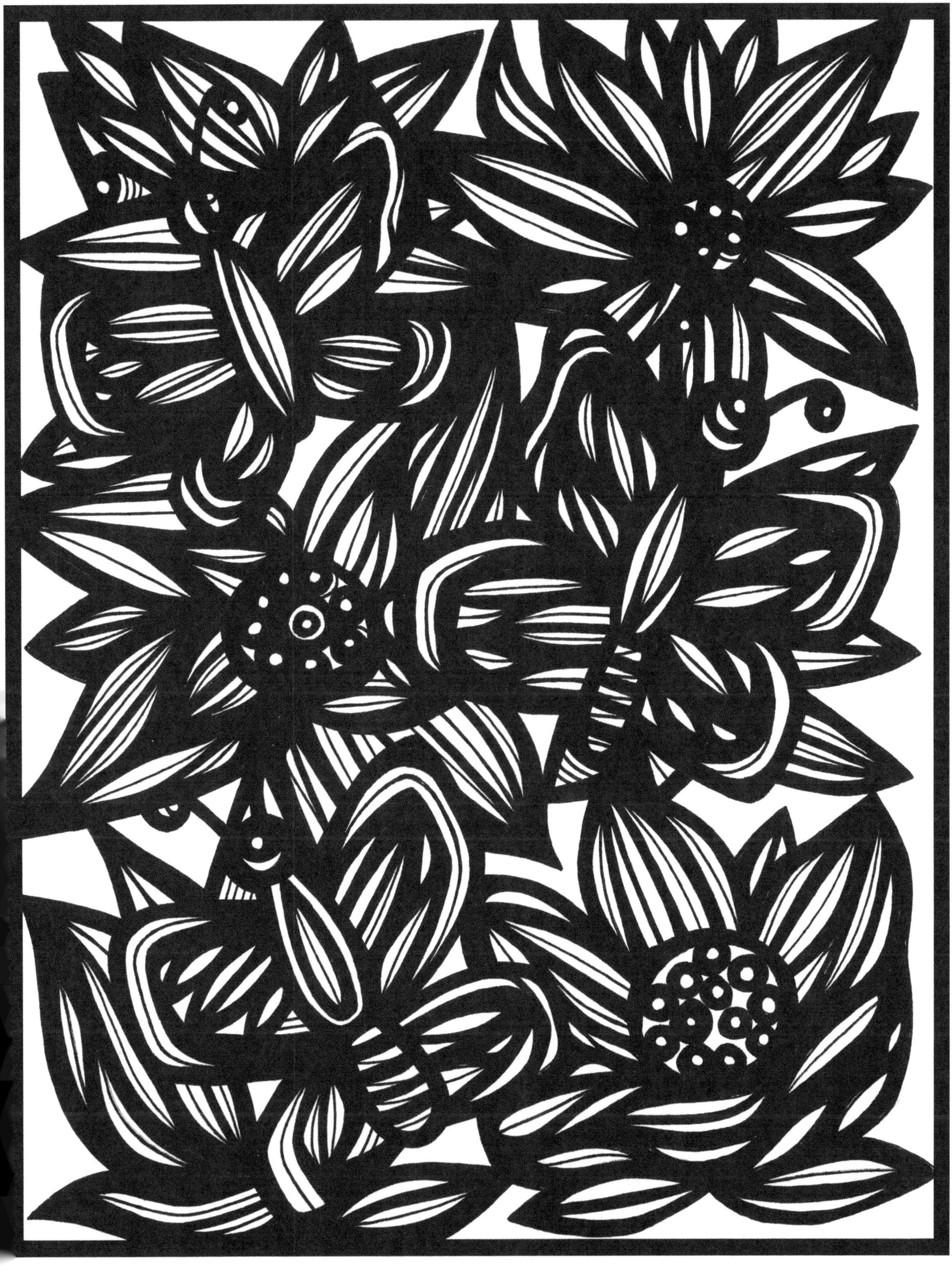

THE END, THANK YOU.

COPYRIGHT 2020
BY EDDIE ALFARO
ALL RIGHTS RESERVED.

MORE BOOKS:
631ART.COM

www.ingramcontent.com/pod-product-compliance
Lightning Source LLC
Chambersburg PA
CBHW080131240526
45468CB00009BA/2351
* 9 7 8 1 7 9 5 6 7 3 6 6 2 *